Bob Mackin

Off the Wall
BASEBALL
TRIVIA

GREY*S*TONE BOOKS
Douglas & McIntyre Publishing Group
Vancouver/Toronto/New York

To the press box gang at Nat Bailey Stadium—
past, present and future.

Greystone Books
A division of Douglas & McIntyre Ltd.
2323 Quebec Street, Suite 201
Vancouver, British Columbia V5T 4S7
www.greystonebooks.com

CANADIAN CATALOGUING IN PUBLICATION DATA
Mackin, Bob, 1970-
    Off the wall baseball trivia

    ISBN 1-55054-821-2

    1. Baseball—Miscellanea. I. Title
GV867.3.M34 2001   796.357   C00-911468-8

Editing by John Eerkes
Cover design by Peter Cocking
Front cover photograph courtesy David Leeds/Allsport
Typeset by Tanya Lloyd/Spotlight Designs
Printed and bound in Canada by Transcontinental Printing
Printed on acid-free paper ∞

We gratefully acknowledge the financial support of the Canada Council for the Arts, the British Columbia Ministry of Tourism, Small Business and Culture, and the Government of Canada through the Book Publishing Industry Development Program (BPIDP) for our publishing activities.

CONTENTS

INTRODUCTION

Baseball is a funny game. A sad game, too. A game that inspires peace. And violence. Simply put, baseball is life.

It touched my life for the first time when I was seven years old. My father took me to my first game at the hometown ballpark, Nat Bailey Stadium. There we saw the new triple A squad, the Vancouver Canadians, play in a most beautiful setting. A German shepherd dog named Baseball Sam was the mascot.

Years later, when my family adopted an orphaned German shepherd, I insisted she be named Sam.

All good things must pass, Baseball Sam and my Sam included. The triple A Canadians, too. But, oh, what days those were! Sometimes weird and wacky.

Like that time in 1988, when a rain-delayed game stretched 19 innings, from June 30 into the wee hours of July 1—Canada's national holiday. After midnight, public address announcer Pat Karl reminded fans that it was indeed Canada Day. Organist Mike Foster took advantage of the inning break to play the national anthem, "O Canada."

The Canadians' manager, Terry Bevington, an American, dutifully stood at attention in the coaches' box on the third base line, doffed his cap and placed it over his heart.

The crowd rose. During the marathon game, the thousands of fans had dwindled to dozens. But the weary and wet choir did the country proud as the maple leaf flag flapped in center field.

Nat Bailey Stadium was also where I saw the San Diego Chicken make mischief and merriment with umpires, players and fans. Max Patkin made merry, too. Like the ballpark, he had seen better days. But he still had some magic to offer as he roamed the diamond and the grandstand in a baggy, old-style uniform, with his red, white and blue cap twisted to one side.

Baseball can also break your heart. As it did on September 17, 1999, when the Canadians won their third Pacific Coast League championship and first at home. It was also the last time they'd play in Vancouver. Eight days later, the C's were triple A World Series champions in Las Vegas. But in the spring of 2000 the pennant, trophy and team went to a newer, shinier, bigger home in Sacramento, California.

Hope springs eternal. On the first weekend of summer 2000, the Canadians of the short-season, single A Northwest League debuted. In the grandstand I spotted a father with his seven-year-old son. May the youngster grow to experience and enjoy the magic of baseball as I did.

BOB MACKIN
January 2001

1

LEADING OFF

Every time a baseball game begins, so does a true adventure. How will it end? Who will win? How many hours and minutes will go by? There's nothing quite like that feeling of uncertainty. Start your adventure through the weird and wild, well-known and unknown of the greatest game on earth with this chapter.

(Answers are on page 5.)

1.1 Many major league greats were born on Christmas Day. Which one is the all-time leadoff home run hitter?
A. Nellie Fox
B. Pud Galvin
C. Rickey Henderson
D. Babe Ruth

1.2 Joel Youngblood began August 4, 1982, with the New York Mets. Which National League team did he end the day with?
A. The Montreal Expos
B. The Philadelphia Phillies
C. The Chicago Cubs
D. The San Diego Padres

1.3 How many home runs did Tommy Thevenow hit out of the park in his career?
A. Zero
B. One
C. 50
D. 250

1

1.4 How many fourth-inning errors did Bob Brenly commit to tie a major league record?
A. Three
B. Four
C. Five
D. Six

1.5 Robin Yount played his entire career with one American League team. His older brother, Larry, did the same in the NL, though for a substantially shorter time. Which team did Larry play for?
A. The Houston Astros
B. The Montreal Expos
C. The Los Angeles Dodgers
D. The St. Louis Cardinals

1.6 At which stadium did Sparky Anderson lose his first game as manager of the NL All-Star team?
A. Tiger Stadium, Detroit
B. Hubert H. Humphrey Metrodome, Minneapolis
C. Riverfront Stadium, Cincinnati
D. Comiskey Park, Chicago

1.7 Dock Ellis claimed to be under the influence of what illicit substance when he pitched a no-hitter in 1970?
A. Heroin
B. PCP (phencyclidine)
C. Cocaine
D. LSD (lysergic acid diethylamide)

1.8 What kind of bird refused to leave the field during game three of the 1933 World Series in Washington, D.C?

A. A bald eagle
B. A seagull
C. A robin
D. A pigeon

1.9 Instead of the number 22, Roger Clemens's World Series ring was incorrectly inscribed with which number?

A. 12
B. 33
C. 4
D. 44

1.10 Pitching prankster Moe Drabowsky gave Bowie Kuhn a "hotfoot" in 1969. Who was Kuhn?

A. The Baltimore Orioles' manager
B. The Minnesota Twins' manager
C. The home plate umpire
D. The commissioner of baseball

1.11 How many rookies were in the Houston Colt .45s lineup on September 27, 1963?

A. None
B. One
C. Five
D. Nine

1.12 Bert Campaneris was the Kansas City Athletics' starting shortstop in 1965. How many other positions did he play on September 8, 1965?

A. One
B. Two
C. Six
D. Eight

1.13 Jimmy Piersall hit just one home run in the NL. How did he celebrate?
A. He ran backwards around the bases
B. He did somersaults and cartwheels
C. He took off his jersey
D. All of the above

1.14 In what month was Carlos May born?
A. January
B. April
C. May
D. September

1.15 What jersey number did Boston Red Sox pitcher Bill "Spaceman" Lee request in 1973?
A. 37
B. 337
C. 73
D. 733

1.16 How many times did Jim Bouton's hat fall off his head during game three of the 1964 World Series?
A. Once
B. Twice
C. 12 times
D. 37 times

1.17 Which of the following was not part of pitcher Mark Fidrych's regular game routine?
A. Talking to baseballs
B. Grooming the pitcher's mound with his hands
C. Throwing a hit baseball back to the umpire
D. Pitching with his cap on backwards

1.18 How many times did New York Yankees' owner George Steinbrenner hire (and fire) manager Billy Martin?
A. Once
B. Twice
C. Five times
D. Ten times

1.19 What color were the balls that Larry MacPhail had the Brooklyn Dodgers use in 1938 and 1939?
A. Yellow
B. Orange
C. Pink
D. White

LEADING OFF
Answers

1.1 **C. Rickey Henderson**
By 1999, there were 64 major leaguers who had been born on December 25. Among them were Nellie Fox, Pud Galvin and Rickey Henderson. But only Henderson managed to hit a major league record 75 leadoff home runs. The Chicago native, born in 1958, is better known as the major leagues' all time base-stealer, with 1,334 through 1999. He debuted with the Oakland Athletics in 1979 and also played with the New York Yankees, New York Mets, Toronto Blue Jays, San Diego Padres, Anaheim Angels and Seattle Mariners.

1.2 **A. The Montreal Expos**
Joel Youngblood made an impromptu road trip on August 4, 1982. He also had base hits 785 miles apart on the same day for different teams. Youngblood was traded from the New York Mets to the Montreal Expos and successfully got on base in both Chicago's Wrigley Field and Philadelphia's Veterans Stadium on

that day. His two-run single in the third inning against the Cubs' Ferguson Jenkins helped New York win 7–4. He left the Windy City to join his new team, the Montreal Expos, in Philadelphia, and arrived in time to enter the game in right field. He hit a single off Phillies pitcher Steve Carlton in the Expos' 5–4 loss.

1.3   A.   Zero

If your team needed a home run hitter, Tommy Thevenow was not the man you'd call. During his 15-year major league career with the St. Louis Cardinals, Pittsburgh Pirates, Cincinnati Reds and Boston Braves, Thevenow hit two regular-season homers—both inside the park, and both in 1926 with the Cardinals. The .247 career hitter never hit a ball over the wall in 4,164 at-bats. Thevenow recorded the most at-bats without a homer (3,347).

1.4   B.   Four

For Bob Brenly, it was the worst of times before it became the best of times. The San Francisco Giants catcher was playing third base on September 14, 1986, when his four errors in the fourth inning gave the Atlanta Braves a 4–0 lead. Brenly couldn't reverse making history, but he decided his team could avoid a loss. So he went to work with his bat. In the fifth inning, he hit a solo home run. He followed with a two-out, two-run single to tie the game at 6–6. Then, with two out in the bottom of the ninth, he smacked a solo home run for the Giants' win. Brenly shares the record with Lew Whistler of the New York Giants (June 19, 1891) and Jimmy Burke of the Milwaukee Brewers (May 27, 1901). Coincidentally, Whistler and Burke also had their four errors in the fourth inning.

1.5   A.   The Houston Astros

Robin Yount played his entire 20-year major league career for the Milwaukee Brewers. In 1999, he was inducted into the Hall of Fame. His older brother, Larry, wasn't so lucky. An eight-year veteran of the Houston Astros' farm system, Larry Yount got his first and only shot on September 15, 1971. He was called to make a relief appearance in the ninth inning against the Atlanta Braves. Yount already had a sore arm, but he didn't tell anyone until he felt too much pain to pitch. He left the mound without facing a batter. It was too late to erase his name from the official scoring record, because the home plate umpire had already indicated the pitching substitution.

DID YOU KNOW?

Robb Nen of the Florida Marlins pitched against the Chicago Cubs' Dave Otto on August 3, 1994. The Marlins were 9–8 winners of the historic pitching match-up. It was the first time that hurlers with palindromic last names faced off. On May 11, 1999, Colorado Rockies left-hander Bobby M. Jones bested New York Mets right-hander Bobby J. Jones 8–5. For the only time in the twentieth century, pitchers who shared the same first and last names met in a game.

1.6   A.   Tiger Stadium, Detroit
Not only was 2000 Hall of Famer Sparky Anderson the first manager to win the World Series in both leagues, he was the first to lose the All-Star Game in both leagues. He managed the NL to a 6–4 loss in the July 13, 1971, game at Tiger Stadium after guiding the Cincinnati Reds to a five-game World Series loss in 1970. Anderson's Reds were back-to-back winners of the fall classic in 1975 and 1976. His first World Series win in the AL came in 1984, as the Tigers beat the San Diego Padres in five games. On July 16, 1985, his AL All-Stars were on the losing end of a 6–1 game at the Hubert H. Humphrey Metrodome in Minneapolis.

1.7   D.   LSD (lysergic acid diethylamide)
Dock Ellis rocketed to fame June 12, 1970 when he pitched a 2–0 no-hitter against the San Diego Padres. He felt euphoric long before the end of the game. Ellis claimed to have pitched while

under the influence of the psychedelic drug LSD. That may explain why he walked eight Padres. Ellis began and ended his career with the Pirates. He also had stops with the New York Yankees, Oakland Athletics, Texas Rangers and New York Mets. In 1977 he played under seven managers on three teams: Billy Martin of the Yankees; Jack McKeon and Bobby Winkles of the Athletics; and Frank Lucchesi, Eddie Stanky, Connie Ryan and Billy Hunter of the Rangers. Ellis concluded his 12-year career where it began, in Pittsburgh as a Pirate. In retirement, he worked as a drug and alcohol rehabilitation counselor.

1.8 D. A pigeon

Did the Washington Senators have pigeon power? If so, it only lasted for game three of the 1933 World Series. On October 5 in Washington, D.C., the Senators hosted the New York Giants. The game was delayed five minutes when a pigeon took up residence on the field. Senators shortstop Joe Cronin and two umpires tried to scare the bird away, but were ignored. Four of Cronin's teammates and a Giants player joined the partially successful second attempt: the bird became airborne but flew back to its original spot on the field. Finally the pigeon flew out of Griffith Stadium, much to the delight of fans, including President Franklin D. Roosevelt. The Senators won the game 4–0, but the Giants won the series in five games.

1.9 B. 33

Talk about ringing the wrong number! When the New York Yankees were presented with their 1999 World Series championship rings on May 29, 2000, pitcher Roger Clemens found that his ring was inscribed with number 33. Clemens wore number 12 for part of his first season with the Yankees, but changed to number 22 in July to match his son Koby's Little League jersey. Clemens debuted in 1984 and won five Cy Young Awards. Not until 1999 did he play on a World Series winner. His game four victory capped a sweep of the NL champions, the Atlanta Braves.

1.10 D. The commissioner of baseball
Pitcher Moe Drabowsky went to greet his former Baltimore Orioles teammates after they swept the Minnesota Twins in the 1969 AL championship series on October 6. Drabowsky, who joined the Kansas City Royals in 1969, also decided he'd give commissioner Bowie Kuhn a surprise. Drabowsky approached baseball's top executive quietly during the trophy presentation, spilled lighter fluid around Kuhn's feet and lit a flame. Kuhn didn't notice the blaze beneath him until his shoes caught fire. That wasn't the last of Drabowsky's hijinks in 1969. During the World Series against the New York Mets, Drabowsky paid a skywriter to send an aerial greeting to the O's and had a boa constrictor sent to their clubhouse.

1.11 D. Nine
The Houston Colt .45s dressed an all-rookie lineup on September 27, 1963, for a game against the New York Mets. Manager Harry Craft's charges lost 10–3 to the Mets, but his players still had 11 hits and two errors. Craft also used six rookie substitutes. Seventeen-year-old starting pitcher Jay Dahl allowed five runs in 2⅔ innings. For the record, the lineup was: left fielder Brock Davis, center fielder Jimmy Wynn, right fielder Aaron Pointer, first baseman Rusty Staub, second baseman Joe Morgan, third baseman Glenn Vaughan, short stop Sonny Jackson, catcher Jerry Grote and Dahl. Of the players, Rusty Staub was the last of the rookie lineup to retire in 1985.

1.12 D. Eight
Bert Campaneris was never as busy during his entire 19-year major league career as he was on September 8, 1965. The Kansas City Athletics sophomore was moved around the field and scorecard to all nine fielding positions by manager Billy Sullivan against the California Angels. However, the Athletics lost 5–3, in 13 innings, and Campaneris didn't make it to the end. He had to leave after a home-plate collision with Angel Ed Kirkpatrick left

him injured in the ninth inning. Campaneris had already earned a spot in baseball history as the first to play all nine positions in a single game. It was also the only time that he pitched. During an inning on the mound, Campaneris allowed one hit, two walks and a strikeout.

DID YOU KNOW?

Cesar Tovar of the Minnesota Twins matched Bert Campaneris's feat on September 22, 1968. In fact, when Tovar took the mound against the Oakland Athletics in the first inning, the first batter he faced was Campaneris, who fouled out. The Twins were 2–1 winners. It didn't happen again until September 6, 2000, at Comiskey Park in Chicago. This time, Texas Rangers utility player Scott Sheldon took only five innings to cover the ballpark. Sheldon was catcher in the fourth, first baseman in the fifth and second baseman in the sixth. He started at right field in the seventh and moved to center field. In the eighth he went from left field to the pitcher's mound after the first out. He fanned the only batter he faced, Jeff Liefer, and then ended the game as third baseman. The Rangers lost 13–1. No National Leaguer has ever played all nine positions in a single game.

1.13 A. He ran backwards around the bases
Jimmy Piersall overcame family hardship and depression to play in the major leagues for 17 years, with the Boston Red Sox, Cleveland Indians, Washington Senators, New York Mets and Los Angeles-California Angels. When he hit his 100th home run on June 23, 1963, Piersall celebrated in a unique way: he ran around the bases backwards at the Polo Grounds. It was his only NL homer. His New York Mets manager, Casey Stengel, wasn't pleased, although fans and the visiting Philadelphia Phillies were amused by his antics.

1.14 C. May

Carlos May wanted everyone to know that he was born on May 17. Below his name on his jersey, May wore number 17, thus becoming the only major leaguer to wear his birthdate in play. The Birmingham, Alabama, native was born in 1948, but the year wouldn't fit on his Chicago White Sox jersey. May spent 1968 to 1975 with the White Sox but was later traded to the New York Yankees and California Angels.

1.15 B. 337

Bill "Spaceman" Lee wanted to change his number 37 to 337 so that his last name could be read upside down. Such was the offbeat philosophy of Lee. The Burbank, California, southpaw was 119–90 in his 14-year career with the Boston Red Sox and Montreal Expos. The ball-playing hippie spoke out against the commercialism of baseball, often feuded with team management and always had something witty to say to reporters; for example, "Baseball is the belly button of America. If you straighten out the belly button, the rest of the country will follow suit." On the eve of the 2000 U.S. presidential election, Lee endorsed Republican George W. Bush. Lee claimed to have once shared marijuana with Bush, a former co-owner of the Texas Rangers.

DID YOU KNOW?

A dozen major leaguers list February 29 as their birthdate, even though it's a day that comes around just every four years: Dickey Pearce (1836), Ed Appleton (1892), Ralph Miller (1896), Roy Parker (1896), Pepper Martin (1904), Al Rosen (1924), Paul Giel (1932), Steve Mingori (1944), Al Autry (1952), Jerry Fry (1956), Bill Long (1960), and Terrence Long (1976). None of baseball's "leap year babies" are in the Hall of Fame.

1.16 D. 37 times

Jim Bouton was a pitcher who became noteworthy because he couldn't keep his mouth shut, nor could he keep his hat on his head when he pitched. Bouton, never afraid to speak his mind, wrote the best-selling *Ball Four,* a tell-all tome about life behind the scenes in the big leagues. It was so controversial that baseball commissioner Bowie Kuhn deemed *Ball Four* "detrimental to baseball." As for his hat, Bouton's full-body throwing style often meant that he'd be reaching down to pick up his cap after a pitch. On October 10, 1964, during his 2–1 game three win for the New York Yankees, an observant reporter noted that Bouton's cap fell off 37 times against the St. Louis Cardinals.

1.17 D. Pitching with his cap on backwards

In the summer of 1976, 22-year-old rookie Mark "The Bird" Fidrych was the toast of the baseball world. The offbeat right-hander who spoke to baseballs and groomed the mound with his hands was truly in love with the game. His curly mane of blond hair, big eyes and six-foot-three frame prompted comparisons to *Sesame Street*'s Big Bird. Fidrych won 11 of his first 13 starts, was the second rookie to start the All-Star Game and finished 19–9 with a 2.34 ERA. The AL rookie of the year was so popular that even the California Angels hosted a Mark Fidrych Autograph Day in Anaheim. However, Fidrych's fame was fleeting. He never returned to his rookie form after he injured his arm in 1977 spring training. He was released after 1981, but tried a comeback with the Boston Red Sox farm system. Tigers fans didn't forget Fidrych. He was given a standing ovation and rounds of thundering applause when he was introduced at Tiger Stadium's closing ceremony in 1999.

1.18 C. Five times

Billy Martin had the ultimate love–hate relationship with New York Yankees owner George Steinbrenner. The last time Steinbrenner fired Martin was on June 23, 1988, when Lou Piniella took over the 40–28 Yankees. Martin had previously succeeded Piniella after the 1985 season. Martin was adept at grabbing headlines for all the wrong reasons. He got in a fistfight in a topless bar in Arlington, Texas, and was suspended for three games for kicking and throwing dirt at umpire Dale Scott. The final straw for Steinbrenner was the team's 2–9 slump, which included three straight one-run losses to the Detroit Tigers. On June 22, New York lost 3–2 to Detroit in ten innings. Piniella assumed Martin's duties and guided the Yankees to a 4–3 win over the Cleveland Indians at home the next day. Martin, the MVP in the 1953 World Series, also managed the Minnesota Twins, Detroit Tigers, Texas Rangers and Oakland Athletics. His greatest triumph was the 1977 Yankees' World Series title.

1.19 A. Yellow
Larry MacPhail's attempt to spread "yellow fever" around baseball didn't fly. The Brooklyn Dodgers' general manager wanted to change the way the game was played (or at least its equipment), so his Dodgers began to use yellow balls. They did so during four games in 1938 and 1939. On August 2, 1938, the Dodgers beat the St. Louis Cardinals 6–2 at Ebbets Field in the first yellow-ball game. The Dodgers employed the colorful cowhide again in 1939, for two losses to the St. Louis Cardinals and one win over the Chicago Cubs.

DID YOU KNOW?

A pair of Texas Rangers went off the wall and inside the park on August 27, 1977, on consecutive pitches. Back-to-back, inside-the-park home runs were hit by Texas Rangers Toby Harrah and Bump Wills in an 8–2 win over New York at Yankee Stadium. Rookie pitcher Ken Clay was the victim (or the culprit, depending on your vantage point).

Game One

CASEY OR YOGI?

You might say Casey Stengel and Yogi Berra were two one-of-a-kind guys. Born 35 years apart in neighboring midwest cities, they both became baseball's most colorful personalities in the pinstripes of the New York Yankees. Off the field, it seemed like they always had something to say—humorous, confusing or both. Decide which of the following facts refer to Casey or Yogi.

(*Answers are on page 120.*)

1. Given name
    A. Charles Dillon _____
    B. Lawrence Peter _____

2. Birthplace and birth date
    A. Kansas City, Missouri, July 30, 1890 _____
    B. St. Louis, Missouri, May 12, 1925 _____

3. Jersey number
    A. 8 (retired by Yankees in 1972) _____
    B. 37 (retired by Mets in 1965 and Yankees in 1970) _____

4. Hall of Fame induction date
    A. 1972 (as a player) _____
    B. 1966 (as a manager) _____

5. Seasons played
    A. 19 _____
    B. 14 _____

6. Position
    A. Outfielder _____
    B. Catcher _____

7. Games played
   A. 2,120 _____
   B. 1,277 _____

8. Home runs
   A. 60 _____
   B. 358 _____

9. Batting average
   A. .284 _____
   B. .285 _____

10. World Series wins as a player
    A. Record ten times _____
    B. Once _____

11. Seasons managed
    A. 25 _____
    B. 7 _____

12. Managerial record
    A. 484–444 _____
    B. 1,905–1,842 _____

13. World Series winners managed
    A. Seven (including a record five consecutive) _____
    B. Zero _____

14. Stengelese or Yogi-isms
    A. "It's deja vu all over again." _____
    B. "The secret of managing is to keep the guys who hate you away from the guys who are undecided." _____
    C. "Good pitching will always stop good hitting, and vice versa." _____

    D. "It ain't over 'til it's over." _____

2

DOUBLE PLAY

People can't live on bread and water alone. Likewise with baseball. Despite the allure of the game, sometimes one needs to look to other sports or pursuits for inspiration and perspiration. Variety is the spice of life, after all. Test your knowledge of the connections between baseball and other pastimes in this chapter.

(*Answers are on page 20.*)

2.1   Deion Sanders played baseball and what other sport as a professional?
   A. Football
   B. Hockey
   C. Boxing
   D. Soccer

2.2   How many games did broadcast mogul and Atlanta Braves owner Ted Turner win during his short career as manager?
   A. None
   B. One
   C. Two
   D. Three

2.3   Moe Berg hit only six career home runs. How many languages could he speak?
   A. One
   B. Three
   C. Six
   D. 12

2.4 In which state did Lou Boudreau play for a professional basketball team in 1939 and 1940?
A. Illinois
B. Indiana
C. Pennsylvania
D. Ohio

2.5 Pitcher Gene Conley was a member of the 1957 World Series champion Milwaukee Braves. For which National Basketball Association team did he help win three consecutive championships?
A. The New York Knicks
B. The Boston Celtics
C. The Chicago Bulls
D. The Minneapolis Lakers

2.6 Which NL team signed Jim Thorpe after his Olympic gold medals were revoked?
A. The Cincinnati Reds
B. The Chicago Cubs
C. The New York Giants
D. The Brooklyn Dodgers

2.7 What kind of degree did George "Doc" Medich study for in his spare time?
A. Law
B. Medicine
C. Psychiatry
D. Zoology

2.8 Which Montreal Canadiens hockey legend did the Montreal Expos honor by wearing his number on their uniforms during 2000?

A. Maurice Richard
B. Ken Dryden
C. Jean Beliveau
D. Howie Morenz

2.9 A TV commercial starring football and baseball star Bo Jackson debuted during the 1989 All-Star Game telecast. What product was being advertised?

A. Louisville Slugger baseball bats
B. Nike cross-training shoes
C. Riddell football helmets
D. Budweiser beer

2.10 Which retired National Basketball Association superstar played for a Chicago White Sox farm team in 1994?

A. Wilt Chamberlain
B. Magic Johnson
C. Kareem Abdul-Jabbar
D. Michael Jordan

2.11 Which "original six" National Hockey League team did National League umpire Bill Stewart coach to a Stanley Cup championship?

A. The Detroit Red Wings
B. The Chicago Blackhawks
C. The Boston Bruins
D. The New York Rangers

2.12 Tony La Russa is baseball's fifth manager who also happens to be a qualified lawyer. How many of the first four are Hall of Famers?

A. One
B. Two
C. Three
D. Four

2.13 Babe Didrikson pitched one inning in major league spring training in 1934. How many Olympic track and field gold medals did she win two years earlier?

A. One
B. Two
C. Three
D. Four

2.14 What was the first ball to hit the scoreboard at Wrigley Field?

A. A baseball
B. A football
C. A golf ball
D. A soccer ball

2.15 John Elway was drafted by which major league team?

A. The Colorado Rockies
B. The San Francisco Giants
C. The Baltimore Orioles
D. The New York Yankees

2.16 Which Hall of Famer was the first to play for the Harlem Globetrotters?

A. Ferguson Jenkins
B. Bob Gibson
C. Lou Brock
D. Satchel Paige

2.17 What was sprinter Herb Washington's duty with the Oakland Athletics?
  A. He played center field
  B. He played shortstop
  C. He was a pitcher
  D. He was a pinch-runner

2.18 In 2000, pitcher John Burkett won money in an event sanctioned by which organization?
  A. The National Association of Stock Car Auto Racing
  B. The Professional Bowlers Association
  C. The Professional Golfers Association
  D. The North American Bullriding Association

DOUBLE PLAY
Answers

2.1   A. Football
"Neon" Deion Sanders became the first major leaguer to hit a home run and score a touchdown in the same week. As a New York Yankee, Sanders homered in a 12–2 win over the Seattle Mariners on Tuesday, September 5, 1989, at the Kingdome. It was the second home run of the season for the left fielder, who was three-for-five with two runs and four RBIs. Five days later, on Sunday, September 10, Sanders returned a punt 68 yards for a touchdown at 5:31 of the first quarter in the Atlanta Falcons' home opener. The Falcons' fifth-round draft pick was one of the highlights of the 31–21 loss to the Los Angeles Rams.

2.2   A. None
Ted Turner built a broadcasting empire in Atlanta, which he later sold to Time Warner. He was married for a time to actress Jane Fonda. But he lost his only game as a major league manager. The owner of the Atlanta Braves sent manager Dave Bristol on a ten-

Did You Know?

Deion Sanders was drafted by the Kansas City Royals, the same team that introduced Heisman Award–winning football player Bo Jackson to the big leagues. Sanders's attempt to be the first to play major league baseball and National Football League games on the same day was spoiled on October 11, 1992. He played for the San Francisco 49ers in Tampa Bay against the Buccaneers in the afternoon and took a charter flight to Pittsburgh for the evening baseball game. He suited up for the Atlanta Braves in game five of the NL Championship Series against the Pirates, but was not called upon by manager Bobby Cox. He may have been helpful in preventing the Pirates from winning 7–1. The Braves eventually won the series in its seventh game, on October 14.

day "scouting" trip after the team lost 16 consecutive games in 1977. Turner was the dugout boss on May 1, when the Braves fell 2–1 to the Pittsburgh Pirates. NL president Charles "Chub" Feeney forbade Turner from managing a second time, citing a rule that prohibits managers and players from having a financial interest in their team. Vern Benson stepped in and guided the Braves to a 6–1 win over Pittsburgh to end the losing streak. Bristol returned, but he was replaced by Bobby Cox before the 1978 season. It wasn't Turner's first run-in with Feeney. In 1976, Turner was reprimanded after signing pitcher Andy Messersmith and issuing him number 17. What got Feeney's goat was Turner's nickname for Messersmith: "Channel." The number and nickname, not a surname, were placed on the back of Messersmith's jersey to read Channel 17. Turner's Atlanta flagship TV station, WTBS, was 17 on the dial.

2.3 D. 12

The word around baseball was that Moe Berg could speak a dozen languages but couldn't hit in any one of them. In fact, he knew how to communicate in twice as many languages (12) as the number of home runs he hit (six) in 13 big league seasons. Berg, a New York native, was shortstop for the baseball team at Princeton University, where he studied seven languages—including Sanskrit—and later joined the Brooklyn Robins in 1923 as back up catcher. He furthered his linguistics studies at Paris's Sorbonne and earned a law degree at New York's Columbia University. He also continued his career in the majors with the Chicago White Sox, Cleveland Indians, Washington Senators and Boston Red Sox. His Japanese-language skills came in handy when he joined Babe Ruth and Lou Gehrig on a barnstorming tour of Japan in 1934. In his spare time, Berg gathered photographs of Japanese factories, shipyards and military facilities for the U.S. government. After his 1939 retirement from the game, he was a spy for the Office of Strategic Services, a predecessor to the Central Intelligence Agency. His fluency in German helped him spy on German nuclear scientists.

2.4 B. Indiana

Lou Boudreau's playing and managing career in the major leagues spanned the years 1938 to 1960. The Cleveland Indians' great was named to the Hall of Fame ten years after retirement. Boudreau also had a brief professional basketball career but wasn't good enough for its hall of fame. In 1939 and 1940, he was a member of the Hammond Ciesar All-Americans, an entry from basketball-mad Indiana to the National Basketball League. The team was last-place in its three-season tenure.

2.5 B. The Boston Celtics

Gene Conley measured six-foot-eight and excelled at both basketball and baseball at Washington State University. As a right-handed, professional baseball pitcher, he went 1⅔ innings in game three of the 1957 World Series, a 12–3 Milwaukee Braves loss to the New York Yankees on October 5. The Braves, however, were winners in the seven-game series. It was Conley's only action in the fall classic during an 11-year major league career. He had better luck in the National Basketball Association playoffs with coach Red Auerbach's Boston Celtics. When the team swept the Minneapolis Lakers in 1959, Conley became the first major leaguer to also win an NBA title. Conley won twice more with the Celtics over the St. Louis Hawks in 1960 and 1961.

2.6 C. The New York Giants

Jim Thorpe was America's greatest male athlete of the first half of the twentieth century and an enduring hero to Native Americans from coast to coast. At the 1912 Olympics in Stockholm, he ran away with records and gold medals in both the pentathlon and decathlon. When Swedish King Gustav V presented Thorpe with his medals, he dubbed Thorpe "the greatest athlete in the world." Thorpe's reply? "Thanks, King." But Thorpe's dream became a nightmare early in 1913, when he was stripped of his gold medals. Olympic officials found out that Thorpe had played minor league baseball in 1909 and 1910 for Rocky Mount and Fayetteville in the class D Eastern Carolina League for about $60 a month. Olympic Games rules at the time restricted participants to pure amateurs. Thorpe resumed his baseball career that season for the New York Giants. Over six seasons, he played 289 NL games for the Giants, Cincinnati Reds and Boston Braves.

He hit seven home runs, had 82 RBIs and a .252 average. He also enjoyed a career in professional football and was named to its hall of fame in 1963, ten years after his death. In 1982, the gold medals were re-awarded to Thorpe posthumously. In a gesture of goodwill, the International Olympic Committee presented replicas to each of Thorpe's seven children.

2.7   B. Medicine
Right-handed pitcher George Medich earned his nickname, "Doc," honestly. He was a medical student at the University of Pittsburgh. The native of Aliquippa, Pennsylvania, also earned a degree in chemistry from the University of Pennsylvania. He put his studies to use at least twice in major league ballparks. As a member of the Pittsburgh Pirates, he climbed into the stands at Philadelphia's Veterans Stadium on April 11, 1976, to help a man who had collapsed from a heart attack. Medich tried in vain to save the 73-year-old man, who was dead on arrival at Methodist Hospital. He had a better result on July 17, 1978, at Baltimore's Memorial Stadium, where he performed heart massage on a 61-year-old fan who suffered a heart attack just before a game between Medich's Texas Rangers and the host Orioles.

2.8   A. Maurice Richard
For the first time in major league history, a team wore the jersey number of a player from a different sport in a show of respect. The Montreal Expos sewed the number 9 of Montreal Canadiens legend Maurice "Rocket" Richard on the right sleeve of their home and away jerseys. Richard, the first player to score 50 goals in 50 games, was hockey's equivalent to Babe Ruth. He was remembered with a moment of silence before a June 2 game between the Expos and Baltimore Orioles at Olympic Stadium. The Hockey Hall of Famer died at age 78 on May 27, 2000, after a battle with cancer. A statue of Richard at Maurice Richard Arena near Olympic Stadium became the site of a makeshift shrine for his thousands of fans.

2.9 B. Nike cross-training shoes

The July 11, 1989, All-Star Game was the "Bo Show" during the game telecast and the commercials. Bo Jackson, a Kansas City Royals outfielder, led off for the American League in the bottom of the first inning with a home run on the second pitch from Rick Reuschel. Wade Boggs followed with a dinger that tied the game at 2–2. Jackson, the left fielder, had made a key running catch in the top of the first inning that forced the NL to strand two runners. The AL won 5–3, and Jackson's two-way play earned him the MVP award. Jackson's play in two different sports prompted Nike to hire him to endorse its cross-training running shoes. A Nike TV commercial starring the part-time Los Angeles Raider premiered during a break in the All-Star Game. It featured Jackson playing football and baseball, then trying his hand at other sports, such as hockey with Wayne Gretzky and basketball with Michael Jordan. The spot ended with Jackson attempting to play guitar with blues legend Bo Diddley. Jackson's career in both sports was never the same after he suffered a hip injury in a 1991 NFL playoff game. In 1993 he became the first major league player with an artificial hip, but retired the following season with the California Angels.

2.10 D. Michael Jordan

Chicago Bulls superstar Michael Jordan hung up his basketball shoes after winning three National Basketball Association championships to pursue a career in baseball in 1994. Jordan went hitless in three at-bats on April 9, 1994, when he made his debut with the Chicago White Sox double-A affiliate Birmingham Barons against the Chattanooga Lookouts. Jordan played outfield and went three-for-20 in 13 spring training games for the White Sox. His season, and career, ended with a .202 average. His hopes of a promotion to the White Sox were dashed when major league players went on strike. Jordan ended his retirement from basketball and returned in 1995 to lead the Chicago Bulls to another three NBA championships before retiring for good in 1999.

2.11 B. The Chicago Blackhawks

Bill Stewart was an NL umpire from 1933 to 1954 who worked four World Series and four All-Star Games. He was behind the plate when the Cincinnati Reds' "Dutch Master," Johnny Vander Meer, pitched a second consecutive no-hitter on June 15, 1938, in Brooklyn. Stewart was one of two referees who officiated the National Hockey League's longest game, a 164-minute, 46-second, six-overtime-period marathon between the Detroit Red Wings and the Montreal Maroons on March 24, 1936. But the native of Fitchburg, Massachusetts, had his name engraved on the Stanley Cup as coach of the 1937–38 Chicago Blackhawks. The Blackhawks upset the Montreal Canadiens and New York Americans before surprising the favored Toronto Maple Leafs in the final series. Chicago held third place in the American Division with a disappointing 14–25–9 regular-season record. The Blackhawks hold the distinction of being the first team with a losing record to win the Stanley Cup.

2.12 D. Four

There really is a clubhouse lawyer. Meet Tony La Russa, the fifth major league manager to also be a qualified attorney. The ex–Chicago White Sox and Oakland Athletics manager won three AL manager of the year awards and has three AL pennants and one World Series title to his credit. The 1978 graduate of the Florida State University law school, who joined the St. Louis Cardinals in 1996, is in good company, because the other four are members of the Hall of Fame. Columbia University graduate John Montgomery Ward was the first. He compiled a 412–320 record from 1880 to 1894 as an NL manager in New York, Brooklyn and Providence and as a Players League manager in Brooklyn. He was inducted into the Hall of Fame in 1964. Baseball's other esteemed team-leading legalists were Hughie Jennings, Miller Huggins and Branch Rickey Sr.

2.13 B. Two
Babe Didrikson was arguably the world's greatest female athlete of the twentieth century. She excelled at tennis, softball, baseball, swimming, golf and track and field. She gained fame when she broke records to win gold medals in javelin and 80-meter hurdles and a silver in high jump at the 1932 Summer Olympics in Los Angeles. On March 20, 1934, before she turned to golf full-time (and co-founded the Ladies' Professional Golf Association), she made an appearance in a spring training game as a pitcher for the Philadelphia Athletics. She allowed no Brooklyn Dodgers hits but walked one batter.

2.14 C. A golf ball
Sam Snead did what Babe Ruth and Ernie Banks couldn't: he hit a ball off the center field scoreboard at Wrigley Field. But Snead's ball was a golf ball. He did it on April 17, 1951, to open the Cubs' home season in a pre-game ceremony. No batted baseball has ever struck the scoreboard. The 27-foot-tall, 75-foot-wide structure is 85 feet above the field. The Cubs beat the Cincinnati Reds 8–3 after Snead's drive. Snead is the PGA Tour's all-time tournament winner, with 81 victories.

2.15 D. The New York Yankees
John Elway was the New York Yankees' first pick in the 1981 draft. He was assigned to the Yankees' New York–Penn League team in Oneonta, south of Cooperstown. In 1982, with the short-season, single-A club, Elway batted .318 and led the team with 24 RBIs. He was the first player chosen by the Baltimore Colts in the 1983 National Football League draft. Elway retired in 1999, after quarterbacking the Denver Broncos to consecutive Super Bowl victories.

2.16 B. Bob Gibson
Before pitcher Bob Gibson spent 17 years as the St. Louis Cardinals ace, the native of Omaha, Nebraska, attended Creighton

University as the first African-American player on its basketball team. He spent the 1957 and 1958 baseball seasons in the minor leagues with Columbus, Omaha and Rochester before joining the Cardinals in 1959. During the off-season he brushed up on his hoop skills as a member of the Harlem Globetrotters, the world-famous barnstorming basketball team. In 1981 he was inducted into baseball's Hall of Fame.

2.17 D. He was a pinch-runner
Herb Washington never appeared at the plate or in a field position for the Oakland Athletics. But he did wear the white, green and yellow uniform and earn a World Series ring in 1974, his rookie season. That didn't sit well with some teammates on the defending, two-time World Series championship team. Washington, a world-class sprinter from Michigan State University, debuted with the A's on April 4, 1974. Club owner Charlie Finley hired him to be the club's "designated runner." The experiment wasn't a success. In Washington's two seasons, he stole only 31 bases and was caught 17 times. Instead of accepting a demotion to the minors, Washington opted to retire. He returned to the professional track and field circuit.

2.18 B. The Professional Bowlers Association
In baseball, John Burkett's pitching target is the catcher's glove. In bowling, it's ten pins. Burkett has five perfect 300-point games to his credit in bowling, but none so far in baseball. His closest was a two-hit outing on April 12, 1996, for the Florida Marlins against the Los Angeles Dodgers. It took him ten years, but he finally won a cash prize in a Professional Bowlers Association Tour event on January 27, 2000. Burkett finished 32nd at the Don Carter Classic in Dallas with a 3,911 score through the qualifying round. He didn't advance to match play, but he did take home a check for $1,040.

DID YOU KNOW?

Bowling has been a popular diversion for ballplayers through the years. Former St. Louis Cardinals Joe Garagiola and Stan Musial opened a bowling center called Redbird Lanes in the Missouri city. Visitors to St. Louis can tour both the St. Louis Cardinals' hall of fame and the International Bowling Museum with the same ticket. A bowling ball belonging to Babe Ruth is on display at baseball's Hall of Fame in Cooperstown, New York.

Game Two

PRESIDENTIAL TRIVIA

Being the most powerful politician in the United States has its privileges—like always being welcome at a ball game. For example, it's a tradition for presidents to throw the ceremonial first pitch at opening day during their term in office. Test your presidential baseball knowledge by matching the names of the presidents in the list with the following "Who am I?" questions.

(Answers are on page 120.)

PRESIDENTS

A. Gerald Ford
B. Harry Truman
C. Bill Clinton
D. Richard Nixon
E. Jimmy Carter

F. Woodrow Wilson
G. John F. Kennedy
H. Franklin D. Roosevelt
I. George Bush
J. William Howard Taft

CLUES

1. _____ I was the first president to toss the ceremonial pitch on opening day, April 14, 1910, at Griffith Stadium in Washington, before the Senators met the Philadelphia Athletics. Who am I?

2. _____ I was the first sitting president to attend a World Series game: the second game of the 1915 fall classic in Philadelphia on October 9 between the Phillies and Boston Red Sox. Who am I?

3. _____ I wrote the famous Green Light letter that allowed baseball to continue during World War II. Two days after my April 12, 1945, death, all major league games were postponed. Who am I?

4._____ I was a switch-pitcher: I threw the opening-day first pitch in 1946 with my left hand. In 1947, I used my right hand. Who am I?

5._____ My grandfather was the mayor of Boston and threw the first pitch at Fenway Park the day it opened in 1912. The home of the Washington Senators was named after my brother, a U.S. senator. Who am I?

6._____ I attended Ted Williams's debut as a manager, an 8–4 New York Yankees win over the Washington Senators on April 7, 1969. Who am I?

7._____ I was vice-president when called upon to "pinch-hit" for another president in the White House. I attended the 1976 All-Star Game. Who am I?

8._____ I never threw out the first pitch at a major league opening day as president, but I did do it twice at Atlanta Braves games while serving as governor of Georgia. Who am I?

9._____ I attended the 1991 All-Star Game at Toronto's SkyDome as guest of Canadian Prime Minister Brian Mulroney. My son was part-owner of the Texas Rangers. Who am I?

10. _____ My wife threw the first pitch on opening day at Wrigley Field in 1994 and joined Harry Caray to sing "Take Me Out to the Ball Game" in the seventh-inning stretch. Who am I?

3

BIG IN THE MINORS

Before a ballplayer can star in "The Show," lots of time is spent in rehearsal. It's called the minor leagues. Though the edges can sometimes be a little rough, the minor leagues offer baseball fans entertainment and an atmosphere that can't be found in the majors anymore. Not only that, but it's a great chance to see the stars of tomorrow, today. Give your minor-league knowledge a test today with these questions.

(Answers are on page 36.)

3.1 The Hawaii Islanders forfeited a triple A Pacific Coast League game to Tacoma in 1976 because the Twins' starting pitcher wore what?
A. Metal cleats
B. Shorts
C. A football helmet
D. No glove

3.2 Members of the PCL's Vancouver Canadians staged a wildcat strike in July 1989 because:
A. They didn't like their uniforms
B. They hadn't received paychecks
C. They disagreed with their manager
D. They weren't allowed to smoke

3.3 Politicians in historic Cooperstown, New York, rejected which minor league's expansion overtures?
A. The Eastern League
B. The International League
C. The Northern League
D. The New York–Penn League

3.4 How many home runs did Justin "Nig" Clarke hit for a single-game record in 1902?
A. Five
B. Six
C. Eight
D. Ten

3.5 Who was the first professional baseball player to hit 60 home runs in a season?
A. Babe Ruth
B. Tony Lazzeri
C. Lou Gehrig
D. Roger Maris

3.6 How old was Joe DiMaggio when he set the baseball record for most consecutive games with a base hit?
A. 17
B. 18
C. 21
D. 27

3.7 In what season was Ila Borders—the first woman to play professional baseball on a men's team—when she retired from the minor leagues?
A. Her first
B. Her second
C. Her third
D. Her fourth

3.8 Which stadium hosted the biggest minor league crowd in history?

A. Municipal Stadium, Cleveland

B. Aloha Stadium, Honolulu

C. B.C. Place Stadium, Vancouver

D. Mile High Stadium, Denver

3.9 The Louisville Redbirds were the first minor league team to draw more than one million fans in a season. Which team was the club's major league affiliate?

A. The Houston Astros

B. The Baltimore Orioles

C. The Cincinnati Reds

D. The St. Louis Cardinals

3.10 The American League beat the National League 2–1 in the 1988 major league All-Star Game in Cincinnati. What was the score in the first triple A All-Star Game played one day later?

A. 2–1

B. 1–0

C. 10–9

D. 5–3

3.11 "Jigger" Statz spent a record number of seasons with the same minor league club. How many years was he with it?

A. Ten

B. 15

C. 18

D. 20

3.12 What was banned in five minor leagues on April 3, 1991?

A. Metal bats

B. Swearing

C. Chewing tobacco and snuff

D. Spitballs

3.13 Denny McLain pitched a no-hitter in his minor league debut. A year later he married the daughter of which Cleveland Indians Hall of Famer?

A. Lou Boudreau

B. Bob Lemon

C. Nap Lajoie

D. Tris Speaker

3.14 Mark McGwire, the major leagues' single-season home run king, played only one full season in the minor leagues. How many home runs did he have?

A. 20

B. 24

C. 26

D. 49

3.15 In what city was Babe Ruth's first home run as a professional?

A. Boston

B. New York

C. Providence

D. Toronto

3.16 Who was the twentieth century's first African-American professional baseball player?

A. Jackie Robinson

B. Larry Doby

C. Satchel Paige

D. Jimmy Claxton

3.17 Marv Foley is the only manager to win a championship in three triple A leagues. Who was his manager when he played for the Chicago White Sox?

A. Tony La Russa

B. Earl Weaver

C. Dick Howser

D. Billy Martin

3.18 For how many seasons was Pam Postema a minor league umpire?

A. One

B. Six

C. Eight

D. 13

BIG IN THE MINORS
Answers

3.1 **A. Metal cleats**

If only he'd changed his shoes. Tacoma Twins starting pitcher Bill Butler violated Aloha Stadium policy by wearing metal spikes on the Astroturf on May 7, 1976. So, stadium staff shut down the outfield floodlights. Home plate umpire Bill Lawson awarded the Twins a 9–0 win over the host Hawaii Islanders half an hour later. The game was supposed to be the first of a seven-game series at the month-old, $32 million, 50,000-seat stadium in Honolulu. Twins manager Cal Ermer argued that it was the policy of the parent Minnesota Twins that pitchers wear metal cleats. He also wondered why such footwear was allowed on Astroturf in major league ballparks in Houston, Cincinnati, Philadelphia and Pittsburgh, but not in the Hawaii state-owned park. Hawaii Governor George Ariyoshi temporarily lifted the ban May 8 so the series could begin with a 4–2 Twins win. The matter was finally resolved when Astroturf manufacturer Monsanto said metal cleats wouldn't negate the warranty.

3.2 **B. They hadn't received paychecks**
The 23 members of the Vancouver Canadians adopted a "no pay, no play" philosophy in Albuquerque on July 6, 1989, and became the first minor league team to strike because their checks were late. The host Dukes were awarded a 9–0 win when the Canadians left the stadium an hour and a half before game time in a show of solidarity against the parent Chicago White Sox. The Canadians' general manager, Brent Imlach—son of legendary National Hockey League coach Punch Imlach—flew from Vancouver to the New Mexico city to deliver the paychecks. When the team resumed play the next day, it registered a convincing 7–3 win over the Dukes. The Canadians would eventually beat the Dukes, the Los Angeles Dodgers' top farm team, in September for the PCL championship.

3.3 **C. The Northern League**
Despite evidence to the contrary, Cooperstown, New York, remains known to many as "the birthplace of baseball." It also remains without a team of its own. That's because on October 26, 1995, the committee that operates Doubleday Field in the central New York village rejected a bid by the six-team, independent Northern League to place one of its two expansion franchises there. Doubleday Field is the site of the annual Hall of Fame Game during induction weekend at the nearby National Baseball Hall of Fame. Village trustee and committee chairman Stuart Taugher explained that Cooperstown "really is not a baseball town, per se, as far as the residents go."

3.4 **C. Eight**
Talk about a career game. Justin "Nig" Clarke had just six home runs in nine major league seasons. But on June 15, 1902, he had eight in a single Texas League game. The Corsicana catcher was eight-for-eight at the plate in his team's overwhelming 51–3 win over Texarkana. The game was played in a small, non-league ballpark in Ennis because Sunday baseball games were not allowed in

Corsicana. Clarke, a 19-year-old from Amherstburg, Ontario, later played in the majors for Cleveland, Detroit, St. Louis Browns, Philadelphia and Pittsburgh.

3.5 B. Tony Lazzeri

Baseball was abuzz in 1925, when Salt Lake City Bees second baseman Tony Lazzeri hit 60 home runs. He also registered 222 RBIs and a .355 batting average. The feat was worthy of applause, although the Pacific Coast League's schedule was a lengthy 197 games. The New York Yankees paid $55,000 and traded five players for Lazzeri. He was worth the investment but was not quite as prolific in 1926, when he hit 18 home runs. In fact, he hit 18 homers three more times, but never exceeded 18 during his 14-year career. He did make more home run history in the majors. For instance, on May 24, 1936, Lazzeri became the first major leaguer to hit two grand slams in one game. And his home run in game two of the 1936 World Series was only the second grand slam in the fall classic. The San Francisco native was inducted posthumously into the Hall of Fame by the veterans' committee in 1991.

3.6 B. 18

Joe DiMaggio was 18 years old and in his second season with the hometown San Francisco Seals of the Pacific Coast League when he hit safely in 61 consecutive games. That same year he also had 28 home runs and a .340 average and led the league with 169 RBIs. DiMaggio's 61st consecutive game with a hit was played on July 25, 1933. Oakland Oaks pitcher Ed Walsh Jr. held DiMaggio hitless the following day to end the streak. DiMaggio joined the Seals in 1932 and played three games after being recruited by his older brother, Vince. In 1935, the New York Yankees sent the Seals $25,000 and five minor leaguers for DiMaggio's rights. He set rookie records in 1936 with 132 runs and 15 triples. His shorter, yet more famous, hitting record began on May 15, 1941. He hit safely in 56 consecutive games until

July 17, when the Cleveland Indians shut him down. DiMaggio, a 1955 Hall of Famer, was an American League All-Star during each of his 13 seasons.

3.7   D.   Her fourth
Ila Borders's retirement from the Zion Pioneerzz on June 29, 2000, wasn't the top sports story of the day. Perhaps it should've been. Borders decided to end her career as the first woman to play professional baseball on a men's team in the middle of her fourth minor league season. In her swan song on June 28, she yielded five hits and three runs in a disappointing 10–6 loss to the Feather River Mudcats. The southpaw's historic debut occurred on May 31, 1997, as a reliever in the sixth inning of a St. Paul Saints Northern League game against the Sioux Falls Canaries. She gave up three earned runs without an out and was the first woman to pitch in a regular-season professional game. She said she wasn't playing the game to break the gender barrier; she simply loved baseball. At the time of her retirement, she was 0–0 and after 8⅔ innings of action in five games. Borders compiled a 2–4 career record in 52 games.

3.8   D.   Mile High Stadium, Denver
The Denver Zephyrs set a minor league attendance record on July 3, 1982, when the American Association team drew 65,666 fans for a game against the Omaha Royals and a fireworks night at Mile High Stadium, which was known as Bears Stadium when it opened in 1948. The Zephyrs moved to New Orleans in 1993, when Mile High Stadium became the temporary home park of the expansion Colorado Rockies. The stadium continued to be the scene of attendance records. The NL newcomers opened the season with a NL regular-season record of 80,227 fans for a game against the Montreal Expos on April 9. By season's end, the Rockies counted 4,483,350 turnstile clicks, the most in a major league season.

3.9   D.   The St. Louis Cardinals

The Louisville Redbirds had a very full nest in 1983. The St. Louis Cardinals' triple A farm team became the first minor league franchise to crack the one million mark in attendance. The millionth fan arrived on August 25, 1983, with two games to go in the home schedule. The final tally for the International League club was 1,052,438. The Redbirds outdrew the Minnesota Twins, Seattle Mariners and Cleveland Indians, the only three major league teams with less than a million at the gate in 1983. The Redbirds were 60,336 shy of the NL's worst draw, the New York Mets. The Cardinals, by comparison, counted a respectable 2,317,914.

DID YOU KNOW?

The first modern triple A World Series was played in 1983 at Louisville, Kentucky. The International League champion Tidewater Tides claimed the title when they won three of their four games against the Denver Zephyrs of the American Association and the Pacific Coast League's Portland Beavers. In 1998, the triple A World Series moved to Las Vegas, where the New Orleans Zephyrs of the PCL beat the IL's Buffalo Bisons in four games.

3.10   A.   2–1

The first triple A All-Star Game was played on July 13, 1988, in downtown Buffalo's Pilot Field. As they had in the major league game the night before, the AL-affiliated all-stars edged the National Leaguers 2–1. This game was enjoyed by 19,500 people at the three-month-old, $43 million ballpark. One of the highlights was a surprise appearance by the notorious Morganna, the "kissing bandit." The ample-breasted blonde woman ran onto the field in the second inning to deliver a smooch to Buffalo Bison player Benny Distefano. Double A didn't get its first all-star game until July 10, 1991, when the AL affiliates beat the NL 8–2 before a crowd of 4,022 at Huntsville, Alabama.

3.11   C. 18
Arnold John "Jigger" Statz, a Waukegan, Illinois, native, died at age 90 on March 16, 1988, in Corona Del Mar, California. He spent a record 18 seasons with the Los Angeles Angels of the Pacific Coast League, making 3,356 hits and a .315 batting average in 2,790 games. He actually began his career in the majors with the New York Giants on July 30, 1919. Over eight seasons in the big leagues, he played 683 games with the Giants, Boston Red Sox, Chicago Cubs and Brooklyn Dodgers. But he seemed to keep coming back to the Angels. He earned the nickname "Jigger" after a type of golf iron; golf was Statz's favorite non-baseball pastime.

3.12   C. Chewing tobacco and snuff
Commissioner Fay Vincent banned chewing tobacco and snuff from the Pioneer, Appalachian, Northwest, New York–Penn and Gulf Coast leagues. Players, coaches, managers, umpires and team personnel were forbidden to use the substances, which were linked to cancer. On June 15, 1993, the ban extended to all other minor leagues affiliated with major league baseball. Travis Baptist was the first player caught breaking the ban and was fined $300 when he was found using snuff on June 26, 1993. The pitcher was on the roster of the aptly named Knoxville Smokies when he was caught with the smokeless tobacco.

3.13   A. Lou Boudreau
At the end of the 1963 season, Denny McLain eloped with Sharyn Boudreau, the daughter of Lou Boudreau, the ex–Cleveland Indians player-manager. McLain debuted on September 21 with the Detroit Tigers and won two of the three games in which he pitched. In his first professional outing, McLain struck out 17 Salem batters en route to a 3–0, no-hit victory for Harlan in a

June 28, 1962, Appalachian League game. McLain's career peaked in 1968 with a 31–6 record. No pitcher since Dizzy Dean in 1934 and no pitcher after 1968 won 30 games in a season. McLain's efforts earned him the Cy Young and MVP awards as the Tigers outlasted the St. Louis Cardinals to win the World Series.

DID YOU KNOW?

O say can you stop fighting? A brawl broke out during a Midwest League game between Cedar Rapids and Kewanee in 1949. Players, fans, umpires and police were involved in the melee, which finally subsided because of the quick thinking of public address announcer Bob Hahn. He played a recording of the "Star-Spangled Banner" loud enough for the throng to pay attention and stand at ease. Soon, peace was restored.

3.14 B. 24

Mark McGwire hit 24 home runs in 138 games for the Oakland Athletics' California League farm team in Modesto in 1985. He debuted with Modesto in 1984 and played 16 games after being drafted tenth overall and seeing action in the Los Angeles Olympics with the U.S. national team. In 1986 he played 151 games with three teams and hit 26 homers. McGwire started the campaign in double A Huntsville, Alabama, where he had ten homers in 55 games. He added 13 with the PCL's Tacoma Tigers in 78 games, before a trio of homers in 18 games with the A's. His power at the plate was finally felt in 1987, when he played 151 games again. This time, he smacked 49 home runs exclusively for the A's—the season's best in the AL. McGwire hit 70 in 1998 for the St. Louis Cardinals to set a new major league record.

3.15 D. Toronto

One of America's greatest sports heroes hit his first home run as a professional in a minor league game in Toronto, Ontario. The historic homer came on September 5, 1914, at Maple Leaf Stadium at Hanlan's Point on Toronto Island. Two Providence Grays were on-base when Ruth hit the ball offered by Toronto Maple Leafs pitcher Ellis Johnson out of the park and into the waters of Lake Ontario. It was Ruth's only home run hit in the International League. Ruth debuted earlier that summer as a pitcher for the Boston Red Sox on July 11 at Fenway Park. The 19-year-old southpaw struck out Jack Graney, the first batter he faced, and allowed Cleveland eight hits in seven innings. The Red Sox were 4–3 winners, but Ruth was not a factor in the decision. On August 5 he was demoted to Providence. His first home run as a major leaguer didn't happen until May 6, 1915, at the Polo Grounds in New York. Yankees pitcher Jack Warhop was his first victim. The Yankees were 5–3 winners.

3.16 D. Jimmy Claxton

You might ask: "Jimmy who?" Canadian-born Jimmy Claxton was the first African-American to play baseball professionally on a Caucasian team in the twentieth century. The native of Wellington, British Columbia, was born on December 14, 1892, to William Claxton, a coal miner with African-American, Indian and French lineage, and Emma Richards, who was from an Irish and English family. They moved to Tacoma, Washington, when Jimmy was three months old. In 1916, 23-year-old Claxton joined the Pacific Coast League's Oakland Oaks. He pitched 2⅓ innings in a May 28 doubleheader, giving up four hits, three runs and four walks. He didn't strike out anyone. His ERA from the day was an unflattering 7.71. But that's not why Claxton never got a chance to redeem himself. He had joined the Oaks by convincing management that he was a Native Indian. The truth eventually became known, and Claxton was released because he was black. He was around long enough, however, for his photograph to be snapped by the Zeenut company for its series of baseball cards—thus becoming the first black ballplayer on a baseball card.

3.17 A. Tony La Russa

Marv Foley's Rochester Red Wings won their tenth Governor's Cup International League championship in 1997 over the Columbus Clippers. The win was Foley's third league championship as a triple A skipper. Foley previously managed the Vancouver Canadians to the 1989 Pacific Coast League championship and the Iowa Cubs to the American Association title in 1993. His major league coaching experience is limited to time with the Chicago Cubs in 1994 and the Baltimore Orioles in 1999. But he did get to play in "the show" between 1978 and 1982, for the Chicago White Sox, as a back-up catcher for manager Tony La Russa.

3.18 D. 13

Pam Postema got to Cooperstown and umpired a major league baseball game. Unfortunately, it was just the 1988 Hall of Fame Game exhibition between the New York Yankees and Atlanta Braves. A year later, the first woman to umpire triple A baseball was out of work. Postema had gone further than Bernice Gera and Christine Wren, women who umped in the low minors during the 1970s but couldn't overcome the sport's old boys network. Postema was hired out of umpiring school in 1977 by the rookie Gulf Coast League. She worked her way through the single A Florida State League and double A Texas League before landing in the triple A Pacific Coast League in 1983. The same year she umped in Cooperstown, she was the home plate arbiter of the triple A All-Star Game in Buffalo. A year after her release, she filed a sexual discrimination lawsuit against the triple A Alliance and major league baseball. It was settled out of court. Postema told her story in the appropriately titled 1992 autobiography, *You've Got to Have Balls to Make It in This League*. After leaving baseball, Postema worked as a courier and factory worker.

Game Three

MINOR LEAGUE MONIKERS

My, oh my! Minor league baseball teams have the most colorful names in all of sport. Match the city (including league and affiliation) with the correct team name, and you'll surely agree.

(Answers are on page 120.)

TEAM NAME

A. Sand Gnats
B. Werewolves
C. Tourists
D. Doubledays

E. Nine
F. Mud Hens
G. Goldeyes
H. Boll Weevils

I. Sounds
J. Sidewinders
K. Pioneerzz
L. Aquasox

M. Greenjackets
N. Lugnuts
O. Curve
P. Quakes

CITY

1. Toledo (AAA International League Tigers) _____
2. Tucson (AAA Pacific Coast League Diamondbacks) _____
3. Nashville (AAA PCL Pirates) _____
4. Altoona (AA Eastern League Pirates) _____
5. Mudville* (A California League Brewers) _____
6. Rancho Cucamonga (A California League Padres) _____
7. Lansing (A Midwest League Cubs) _____
8. Asheville (A South Atlantic League Rockies) _____
9. Piedmont (A South Atlantic League Phillies) _____
10. Augusta (A South Atlantic League Red Sox) _____
11. Savannah (A South Atlantic League Rangers) _____
12. Everett (A Northwest League Mariners) _____
13. Winnipeg (independent Northern League) _____
14. London (independent Frontier League) _____
15. Zion (independent Western Baseball League) _____
16. Auburn (A New York–Penn League Astros) _____

*Based in Stockton, California.

4

THE INTERNATIONAL PASTIME

Baseball has taken root right around the globe. Wherever there is green grass, there seems to be a diamond—whether it's Australia, Israel or even Russia. Baseball is no longer the exclusive dominion of Americans. In fact, some of the best players in the game today are foreigners. Test your worldwide knowledge in this chapter.

(*Answers are on page 50.*)

4.1 Former Milwaukee Brewers catcher Dave Nilsson owns a baseball league in his native country. Where was he born?
A. Australia
B. Norway
C. Sweden
D. Iceland

4.2 Who was the first Japanese-born major leaguer?
A. Hideki Irabu
B. Mac Suzuki
C. Hideo Nomo
D. Masanori Murakami

4.3 Olaf "Swede" Henriksen was the first Scandinavian-born player to appear in a World Series game. What country was he from?
A. Sweden
B. Denmark
C. Norway
D. Finland

4.4 American League umpire Jim McKean, a Canadian, played which professional sport in his home country?
A. Hockey
B. Lacrosse
C. Football
D. Basketball

4.5 Which future National League manager was the only player in the lineup both times Babe Ruth's career home run mark was broken?
A. Davey Johnson
B. Dusty Baker
C. Darrell Evans
D. Phil Niekro

4.6 What was the name of the space shuttle on which the ceremonial first pitch in game five of the 1995 World Series was thrown?
A. *Columbia*
B. *Atlantis*
C. *Challenger*
D. *Enterprise*

4.7 Bobby Thomson, who hit the famous "shot heard 'round the world," was born in which Scottish city?
A. Airdrie
B. Glasgow
C. Dundee
D. Edinburgh

4.8 In which city did Chicago Cub Shane Andrews hit the first home run of 2000?

A. Toronto

B. Tokyo

C. Monterrey

D. Sydney

4.9 Where was the major leagues' first regular-season opening game south of the United States?

A. Mexico City

B. Tijuana

C. Monterrey

D. Mazatlan

4.10 Much-traveled Jose Canseco was a member of which team when he became the first foreign-born player to hit 400 home runs?

A. The Tampa Bay Devil Rays

B. The Toronto Blue Jays

C. The Oakland Athletics

D. The New York Yankees

4.11 How many national baseball halls of fame is Cuban legend Martin Dihigo a member of?

A. One

B. Two

C. Three

D. Four

4.12 Which of the following players was not born in San Pedro de Macoris, Dominican Republic?

A. Sammy Sosa

B. George Bell

C. Pedro Martinez

D. Tony Fernandez

4.13 What was the margin of victory in the Montreal Expos' first away game and first home game?

A. One run

B. Two runs

C. Six runs

D. Ten runs

4.14 A Canadian played third base in the first AL regular-season game outside the United States. He was also the first-base coach for the St. Louis Cardinals when Mark McGwire broke Roger Maris's single-season home run record. Who is he?

A. Ferguson Jenkins

B. Dave McKay

C. Larry Walker

D. Doug Frobel

4.15 In 1995, Cal Ripken Jr. set major league baseball's record for consecutive games played. In what year did he set the world record?

A. 1994

B. 1995

C. 1996

D. 1997

4.16 Who was the first Latin American inducted into the National Baseball Hall of Fame?

A. Martin Dihigo

B. Roberto Clemente

C. Orlando Cepeda

D. Tony Perez

4.17 Which major league team played the Cuban national team in a home-and-home exhibition series in 1999?
A. The Houston Astros
B. The Tampa Bay Devil Rays
C. The Florida Marlins
D. The Baltimore Orioles

THE INTERNATIONAL PASTIME
Answers

4.1 **A. Australia**
Dave Nilsson is a man who comes from Down Under—Brisbane, Australia, to be precise. He bought International Baseball League Australia for $3.5 million in 1998 and became chairman of the six-team circuit, which runs from December through mid-February. Under Nilsson, wooden bats replaced metal and nine-inning games became the rule in the IBLA. Nilsson made his major league debut with the Milwaukee Brewers on May 18, 1992, and played in the 1999 All Star Game for the NL. He said "G'day" to the Brewers at season's end so that he could split his time between the Chunichi Dragons in Japan and the Australian Olympic team.

4.2 **D. Masanori Murakami**
Masanori Murakami was the first major leaguer from "the land of the rising sun." The left-handed pitcher and native of Otsuki, Japan, was signed by the San Francisco Giants along with third baseman Tatsuhiko Tanaka and catcher Hiroshi Takahashi. The three high school stars affiliated with the Nankai Hawks of Japan's Pacific League were assigned to the Giants' California League farm team in Fresno. On September 1, 1964, Murakami was with the parent club and kept the New York Mets off the scoreboard during a one-inning relief appearance in a 4–1 Giants loss. Murakami compiled a 5–1 record in 54 games over the next two seasons before he returned to Japan for good.

4.3 **B. Denmark**

Although Olaf Henriksen was nicknamed "Swede," he was actually a Dane, born in Kirkerup, Denmark. The outfielder played seven seasons with the Boston Red Sox, beginning in 1911. He appeared in two games of the 1912 World Series against the New York Giants, doubling in his only at-bat as a pinch-hitter. He was used sparingly again when the Red Sox won back-to-back World Series titles in 1915 and 1916 against the Philadelphia Phillies and Brooklyn Robins.

4.4 **C. Football**

Jim McKean went from three downs to three strikes. The former Canadian Football League quarterback and kicker became an AL umpire in 1974. McKean, a Montrealer, helped kick the Saskatchewan Roughriders to a 29–14 win over the Ottawa Rough Riders in the 1966 Grey Cup championship game in Vancouver. He shares the distinction of being the first Canadian to umpire in the World Series with Paul E. Runge of St. Catharines, Ontario. Runge, an NL umpire from 1973 to 1997, was on the crew with McKean for the 1979 fall classic between the Pittsburgh Pirates and Baltimore Orioles. McKean continued to umpire until 1998.

4.5   A. Davey Johnson

Davey Johnson ended his major league career with just 136 home runs, but he witnessed two players break Babe Ruth's career home run record. Johnson was in the Atlanta Braves' lineup when Hank Aaron hit his 715th home run in 1974. Two years later, Johnson was playing in Japan with Tokyo's Yomiuri Giants when teammate Sadaharu Oh hit his 715th. Aaron retired with 755, but Oh became the all-time champion when he hit his 756th on September 3, 1977. He eventually retired with 868 in 1980. Johnson's best year was 1973, when he led the Braves with 43 homers, which was three more than Aaron's total that year and a record for second basemen. Johnson managed the 1986 World Series–winning New York Mets.

4.6   A. *Columbia*

Out of this world! Baseballs were part of the payload on the Space Shuttle *Columbia* in a 1995 mission to research microgravity. The balls traveled 6.6 million miles for 15 days, 21 hours, 53 minutes and 16 seconds on the orbiter. Commander Kenneth Bowersox threw the ceremonial first pitch for game five of the 1995 World Series a day early aboard *Columbia*. Footage was beamed to earth and shown on TV just before the start of the October 26 game, a 5–4 Cleveland Indians win over the Atlanta Braves. It took seven tries for Bowersox and his crewmates to get it right. Said Bowersox: "To the Braves and to the Indians, good luck in game five of the World Series. Now let's play ball!" The Braves went on to win the series in six games. One of the balls is on display in the Hall of Fame in Cooperstown. The other is at NASA's Lewis Research Center in Cleveland.

4.7   B. Glasgow

New York Giants great Bobby Thomson was born in Glasgow, Scotland, and was dubbed the "Staten Island Scot." He is best known for "the shot heard 'round the world": the ninth-inning, three-run homer on October 3, 1951, that gave the Giants a 5–4 come-from-behind win and the NL championship over the Brooklyn Dodgers. As the ball flew over the Polo Grounds fence, flabbergasted play-by-play announcer Russ Hodges spoke for all Giants fans when he shouted "the Giants win the pennant!" into his microphone five times. The win was the culmination of baseball's greatest comeback. The Giants won 37 of their last 44 games to pull even with the Dodgers at 96–58 and force the three-game tiebreaker. Thomson and the Giants appeared emotionally spent in the six-game World Series loss to the New York Yankees.

4.8 **B. Tokyo**

"Sayonara, baseball!" Shane Andrews's home run on March 29, 2000, was the first home run after the 1900s and the first regular-season homer hit in Asia. The Chicago Cubs and New York Mets participated in the earliest opening day ever in the Tokyo Dome as Japanese Crown Prince Naruhito and Princess Masako watched from the Royal Box. The Cubs beat the Mets 5–3 on the strength of Andrews's two-run homer in the seventh inning off the Mets' Dennis Cook. When the Mets beat the Cubs 5–1 in 11 innings to achieve a split, New York pinch-hitter Benny Agbayani hit the first grand slam of the new season off Danny Young to break a 1–1 tie.

DID YOU KNOW?

Hideo Nomo was the first Japanese pitcher to throw a major league no hitter. He made history at Coors Field in Denver, shutting down the heavy-hitting Colorado Rockies 9–0 on September 17, 1996. Hideki Irabu and Mac Suzuki registered another first on May 7, 1999, when they became the first Japanese pitchers to start a major league game against each other. Irabu pitched the New York Yankees to a 10–1 win at Yankee Stadium over Suzuki and the Seattle Mariners.

4.9 C. Monterrey

Tortillas and cerveza were on the menu when the San Diego Padres hosted the Colorado Rockies on April 4, 1999, in the first major league baseball season opener outside the United States or Canada. The Rockies beat the Padres 8–2. It wasn't the first time Estadio Monterrey was a major league venue. On August 16, 1996, the Padres won 15–10 to start a three-game series with the New York Mets. The Mets evened the series with a 7–3 win, but the Padres—led by Mexican-born, left-handed pitcher Fernando Valenzuela—won the final game 8–0. Valenzuela was the first pitcher to win rookie of the year and Cy Young honors, with the 1981 World Series champion Los Angeles Dodgers.

4.10 A. The Tampa Bay Devil Rays

Jose Canseco's 400th career home run came in a Tampa Bay Devil Rays jersey on April 14, 1999, against the Toronto Blue Jays at the SkyDome. Canseco, a Havana, Cuba, native, played in Toronto the previous season and hit a career-best 46 home runs. He broke into the majors in 1985 with the Oakland Athletics.

4.11 D. Four

Martin Dihigo, Cuba's greatest baseball export, is the only player inducted into the national baseball halls of fame in four countries: the United States, Cuba, Mexico and Venezuela. His induction into Cooperstown occurred in 1977, albeit in the Negro leagues' category. A native of Matanzas, Dihigo played every position during his 30-year career, which peaked in 1937 and 1938. On September 16, 1937, he pitched the first professional no-hitter in Mexico, a 4–0 victory over Nogales in Veracruz. He also had an unprecedented six-for-six day at the plate on September 18, 1938, for Veracruz against Agrario. That year Dihigo led the Mexican League with an 18–2 record and a 0.90 ERA. Fidel Castro rewarded the national hero for his patriotism by appointing Dihigo as Cuba's minister of sports, a post he held until his death in 1971.

4.12 C. Pedro Martinez

Pitcher Pedro Martinez is a native of Manoguayabo, Dominican Republic. He made All-Star Game history when he struck out the first four NL batters in the 1999 mid-summer classic before fans of his Boston Red Sox at Fenway Park. The three-time Cy Young Award winner debuted with the Los Angeles Dodgers as a reliever on September 24, 1992, and was traded to the Montreal Expos in time for the 1994 season. Pedro was reunited with older brother Ramon Martinez (who was born in Santo Domingo, Dominican Republic) in 1999 on the Boston Red Sox.

4.13 A. One run

The Montreal Expos, the first non-American major league team, were 11–10 winners in their inaugural game on April 8, 1969, against the Mets at Shea Stadium in New York. Bob Bailey's two-run double in the first was the team's first hit. When the Expos debuted at home on April 14—the first major league regular season game outside the United States—they edged the St. Louis Cardinals 8–7 at Jarry Park. The NL expansion team finished 52–110 in its first season.

4.14 B. Dave McKay

The AL expansion Toronto Blue Jays opened their first season at home on April 7, 1977, at Exhibition Stadium before 44,649 people. The third baseman was a Canadian—Vancouverite Dave McKay. McKay played three years with the Blue Jays when he was claimed off the Minnesota Twins in the expansion draft prior to the 1977 season. He spent the final three years of his career with the Oakland Athletics and became a coach in 1984. He served under manager Tony La Russa in both Oakland and St. Louis. At Busch Stadium on September 8, 1998, McKay reminded a jubilant Mark McGwire to touch first base after hitting his record-breaking 62nd home run of the season.

4.15 C. 1996

Cal Ripken Jr. surpassed American "ironman" Lou Gehrig in Baltimore on September 6, 1995, when he played his 2,131st game in a row. That was the North American record. On June 14, 1996, Cal Ripken Jr. played his 2,216th consecutive game against the Kansas City Royals to break the world record set in Japan by Sachio Kinugasa. Kinugasa played 2,215 consecutive games until his retirement at age 40 on October 22, 1987, with the Hiroshima Carp in the Central League. Ripken's streak ended at 2,632 when he voluntarily sat out a game on September 20, 1998, and was replaced by Ryan Minor.

4.16 B. Roberto Clemente

The Brooklyn Dodgers signed Puerto Rican Roberto Clemente in 1954 and sent him to their triple A team in Montreal. He returned to Puerto Rico only to be re-drafted by Pittsburgh Pirates general manager Branch Rickey, the former Dodgers boss. Clemente joined the Pirates in right field and spent his entire 18-year career in the Pennsylvania city, where he helped win World Series championships in 1960 and 1971. He compiled exactly 3,000 hits and a .317 batting average through the 1972 season. When a December 1972 earthquake killed 6,000 people in Nicaragua, Clemente began a relief effort to help the thousands of homeless and injured. On New Year's Eve, he rented a DC-7 cargo plane to deliver supplies from Puerto Rico to

---

DID YOU KNOW?

In September 2000, the Hall of Fame in Cooperstown, New York, replaced Roberto Clemente's plaque to correct his name. When he was inducted in 1973, the plaque had his mother's maiden name and father's last name in the wrong order. Instead of Roberto Walker Clemente, the new plaque reads Roberto Clemente Walker. According to Latin American tradition, the maiden name of a person's mother follows the surname.

Nicaragua. The mercy flight ended in tragedy when it crashed into the ocean. The Hall of Fame waived its traditional five-year waiting period and Clemente was elected to the shrine posthumously in 1973.

4.17 D. The Baltimore Orioles

The Baltimore Orioles and Cuban national team played a historic home-and-home exhibition series in 1999—almost 40 years after the professional Havana Sugar Kings of the U.S.-based triple A International League moved to the mainland. On March 28, at Estadio Latinoamericano in Havana, the Orioles were 3–2 winners in 11 innings. When the friendly series shifted to Baltimore's Camden Yards, the Cubans doubled the Orioles 12–6. The Sugar Kings reigned in Havana from 1954 to 1959. Fidel Castro's revolution caused the 1959 IL champions to relocate during the 1960 season to Jersey City, New Jersey. Havana baseball fans didn't get a chance to see their team defend the 1959 Junior World Series title, which the Sugar Kings won in seven games over the visiting American Association champion Minneapolis Millers.

DID YOU KNOW?

Cuban leader Fidel Castro made an appearance on the mound on July 24, 1959, for an army pickup team called Los Barbudos ("the bearded ones") against military police officers at Havana's El Cerro Stadium. The exhibition preceded a match between the Rochester Red Wings and Havana Sugar Kings. Castro struck out two batters in two innings.

Game Four

RETIRED JERSEY NUMBERS

A major league player's jersey number was retired from both the American League and the National League in 1997. Unscramble the last names of these players whose jerseys have been retired, and arrange the highlighted letters to spell the name of the player whose jersey was retired. Add the jersey numbers listed to get the player's career batting average. Finally, subtract by 269 for the jersey number of the mystery Hall of Famer.

(Answers are on page 120.)

Reggie SNOCKAJ 44 (Yankees)

Ernie SABNK 14 (Cubs)

Roberto LECENMTE 21 (Pirates)

Lou BORCK 20 (Cardinals)

Harold SNAIBE 3 (White Sox)

Willie GARSTELL 8 (Pirates)

Hank RANAO 44 (Braves)

Larry BYDO 14 (Indians)

Frank BRINSONO 20 (Orioles)

Tony ALIVO 6 (Twins)

Joe GORMAN 8 (Reds)

Willie SYAM 24 (Giants)

Don LINSOW 40 (Astros)

Bob BIGSON 45 (Angels)

5

FRANKLY BALLPARKS

Baseball stadiums are more than just seats arranged around a diamond.
They're a home away from home for young and old, male and female.
They're cathedrals where one can go for peace of mind. Or they can be
raucous "bins of din." Outdoors or indoors, no two ballparks are alike.
Explore their differences in the following pages.

(Answers are on page 63.)

5.1 Whose initials are displayed vertically in Morse code on the
hand-operated scoreboard at Boston's Fenway Park?
A. Babe Ruth
B. Tom A. Yawkey and Jean R. Yawkey
C. Carlton Fisk
D. Ted Williams

5.2 Which city's American League ballpark was built with a giant
letter A beyond the outfield fence?
A. Atlanta
B. Anaheim
C. Oakland
D. Arlington

5.3 A body of water beyond right field at San Francisco's Pacific
Bell Park is named after what former Giant great?
A. Willie McCovey
B. Willie Mays
C. Orlando Cepeda
D. Vida Blue

5.4 Among the plaques at Yankee Stadium's Monument Park are two that honor non-baseball people. Who are they?

A. Presidents Ronald Reagan and George Bush

B. New York City mayors Ed Koch and Rudolph Giuliani

C. Pope Paul VI and Pope John Paul II

D. Rock musicians Billy Joel and Bruce Springsteen

5.5 Which river does not flow past Three Rivers Stadium in Pittsburgh?

A. The Ohio River

B. The Monongahela River

C. The Allegheny River

D. The Mississippi River

5.6 On April 20, 1912, new ballparks opened in Detroit and Boston. News of what historic event overshadowed the occasion?

A. The sinking of the *Titanic*

B. The beginning of World War I

C. The first automobile rolling out of the Ford plant

D. Woodrow Wilson winning the U.S. presidency

5.7 Which major league ballpark was the first to have permanent lights for evening games?

A. Shibe Park

B. Ebbets Field

C. Crosley Field

D. Comiskey Park

5.8 Wrigley Field in Chicago was the last ballpark to install lights. In what year was Wrigley Field lit?

A. 1941

B. 1969

C. 1986

D. 1988

5.9   Which sunny city's ballpark went the longest without a rainout?
   A. Miami
   B. Los Angeles
   C. Anaheim
   D. San Diego

5.10   What team provided the opposition for the final home games in New York's two National League ballparks in 1957?
   A. The St. Louis Cardinals
   B. The Philadelphia Phillies
   C. The Pittsburgh Pirates
   D. The Cincinnati Reds

5.11   What was buried behind the center field fence at Cleveland Stadium on September 23, 1949?
   A. An Indians jersey
   B. An Indians cap
   C. The Indians' 1948 AL pennant
   D. A ceremonial peace pipe

5.12   Which major league ballpark was the temporary home of a National Hockey League expansion franchise before an AL team moved in?
   A. The SkyDome, Toronto
   B. Bank One Ballpark, Phoenix
   C. Hubert H. Humphrey Metrodome, Minneapolis
   D. Tropicana Field, St. Petersburg

5.13   What was special about Mark Grace's May 12, 1998, home run at Bank One Ballpark in Phoenix?
   A. It was inside the park
   B. It went through the roof
   C. It landed in a swimming pool
   D. It was a grand slam

5.14 Where did the first rainout of an indoor baseball game occur in the major leagues?

A. Toronto

B. Seattle

C. Minnesota

D. Houston

5.15 The Minnesota Twins won the first indoor World Series in seven games in 1987. How long was the second indoor World Series in 1991?

A. Four games

B. Five games

C. Six games

D. Seven games

5.16 How many World Series games did Cy Young win at Boston's Huntington Avenue Baseball Grounds in 1903?

A. None

B. One

C. Two

D. Three

5.17 Which stadium did a team owner call "the eighth wonder of the world"?

A. Dodger Stadium

B. The SkyDome

C. Yankee Stadium

D. The Astrodome

5.18 Willie Mays was chosen MVP in the first indoor All-Star Game. Which injured player did he replace?

A. Pete Rose

B. Roberto Clemente

C. Orlando Cepeda

D. Ernie Banks

5.19 How many seconds did it take for Seattle's Kingdome to implode on March 26, 2000?

A. 10.5

B. 16.8

C. 30

D. 60

FRANKLY BALLPARKS

Answers

5.1 **B.** **Tom A. Yawkey and Jean R. Yawkey**

The Yawkeys are gone, but their memory lives on at Fenway Park's hand-operated scoreboard. The initials of the former Boston Red Sox owners are displayed there in Morse code. Tom Yawkey and Eddie Collins, a 25-year major leaguer, bought the AL franchise from Bob Quinn in 1933. After Yawkey's death in 1976, his widow Jean took over the franchise and controlled it until she died in 1992. The vertical combinations of dots and dashes on the field-level scoreboard honor the couple subtly; some might say subliminally. If you look closely at the bottom of the 37-foot "Green Monster" left field wall, you'll see: . _ _ _   . _ .   _ . _ _ (JRY) and _ . _ _ . _ _ (TAY). The Red Sox won the AL pennant only three times during Tom Yawkey's ownership (1946, 1967, and 1975). He was inducted into the Hall of Fame in 1980.

5.2 **B.** **Anaheim**

Now that's a vowel! A giant rendering of the California Angels' "halo-A" logo stood behind the left field fence at Anaheim Stadium for 24 years. The 230-foot-tall, $1 million "A" supported the scoreboard and was erected by sponsor Standard Oil. The $24 million, 43,250-seat stadium (now called Edison International Field of Anaheim) opened on April 9, 1966. The big A was moved to the edge of the parking lot in 1980 when the stadium was renovated to accommodate the NFL's Los Angeles Rams.

5.3 A. Willie McCovey

When Pacific Bell Park opened in 2000 on the shores of San Francisco Bay, the Giants named a body of water immediately beyond the right field wall McCovey Cove. Willie McCovey was inducted into baseball's Hall of Fame in 1986. He hit the most home runs at the Giants' previous home, Candlestick Park (231) and played the most seasons at first base in major league history (22). The 40,800-seat, $319 million Pacific Bell Park saw its first regular-season game on April 11, 2000, when the Giants hosted the Los Angeles Dodgers. It's located, appropriately enough, at 24 Willie Mays Plaza.

5.4 C. Pope Paul VI and Pope John Paul II

You don't have to be a Yankee to be honored in Yankee Stadium's Monument Park beyond the outfield fence. But being a Pontiff helps. Two Roman Catholic popes, Paul VI and John Paul II, are among those with plaques in the outdoor shrine to Yankee legends. The two popes performed mass for New York worshippers at Yankee Stadium during American tours. Yankee Stadium opened on April 18, 1923, when Babe Ruth homered in a 4–1 win over his former team, the Boston Red Sox. Winning pitcher Bob Shawkey allowed three hits. Shawkey returned to Yankee Stadium on April 15, 1976, to throw the ceremonial first pitch when the House That Ruth Built reopened after a two-year, $45 million renovation. The Yankees beat the Minnesota Twins

---

DID YOU KNOW?

The other honorees in Yankee Stadium's Monument Park are Lou Gehrig, Miller Huggins, Babe Ruth, Joe DiMaggio, Mickey Mantle, Ed Barrow, Jacob Ruppert, Casey Stengel, Joe McCarthy, Thurman Munson, Billy Martin, Whitey Ford, Lefty Gomez, Roger Maris, Allie Reynolds, Elston Howard, Phil Rizzuto, Bill Dickey, Yogi Berra, Reggie Jackson and Don Mattingly.

11–4 before 52,613 fans, who were glad to see the Bronx Bombers return after two years as guests of the Mets at Shea Stadium in Queens.

5.5   D. The Mississippi River
Pittsburgh's Three Rivers Stadium opened on July 16, 1970, near the confluence of the Ohio, Monongahela and Allegheny rivers. The stadium's site is a former island that also served as a Native burial ground. The circular stadium with artificial turf was built for $35 million and seated 47,972. The Pirates moved in 2001 to PNC Park, a $209 million natural grass, baseball-only facility with seating for 38,000.

5.6   A. The sinking of the *Titanic*
The supposedly unsinkable luxury cruise liner *Titanic* collided with an iceberg in the North Atlantic southeast of Newfoundland on the night of April 14, 1912. It sank two and a half hours later. The ill-fated maiden voyage of the British ship from Southampton, England, to New York City ended with 1,517 passengers dead. A joint French–American expedition found the wreckage on the ocean's floor in 1985. The disaster captivated the imagination of generations and was the subject of the 1997 blockbuster movie *Titanic*. As news of the tragedy spread through North America, Fenway Park in Boston and Navin Field (a.k.a. Tiger Stadium) in Detroit opened on April 20. The Red Sox beat the New York Yankees 7–6 in 11 innings. The Tigers had a similar one-run victory, 6–5, over the Cleveland Indians, also in 11 innings.

5.7   C. Crosley Field
A bright, new era in major league baseball began on May 24, 1935, when 20,422 fans descended on Crosley Field in Cincinnati. President Franklin D. Roosevelt pushed a telegraph key from the White House that illuminated a light on a field-level desk, where Cincinnati Reds general manager Larry MacPhail was

waiting. MacPhail then flipped a switch that turned on 632 lights at Crosley Field. The Reds proceeded to edge the Phillies 2–1.

5.8   D. 1988

Let there (finally) be light! Chicago's Wrigley Field was the last stadium in the major leagues to install floodlights. Although Cubs owner Philip K. Wrigley had lights ready for installation, he donated them to the World War II effort on December 8, 1941 (the day after Japan attacked Pearl Harbor). The park was dark until August 8, 1988, when the Cubs met the Philadelphia Phillies. The historic game was rained out after three and a half innings. So the first official night game at the "Friendly Confines" happened a day later, on August 9, when the Cubs upended the New York Mets 6–4. Wrigley Field had actually hosted its first nighttime baseball game 45 years earlier, when a portable system was used to illuminate the All-American Girls Professional Baseball League all-star game on July 1, 1943.

5.9   D. San Diego

Mother Nature smiled on the San Diego Padres for more than 15 years. In fact, you didn't need an umbrella if you visited Jack Murphy Stadium for a Padres game during the decade and a half "rainout drought." After an April 20, 1983, postponement, the Padres didn't suffer another until May 12, 1998, when a scheduled meeting with the New York Mets was a washout. The game was postponed 96 minutes after the scheduled 7:05 P.M. first pitch, ending the streak at 1,173 home dates. Not all the games were in San Diego, however. The Padres played three "home" games in Monterrey, Mexico, on August 16–18, 1996, and another two in Honolulu, Hawaii, on April 19–20, 1997. The former games were moved south because San Diego was hosting the Republican National Convention; the latter were moved to the mid-Pacific because the Padres' home ballpark was being renovated.

5.10　C.　The Pittsburgh Pirates

Only 6,702 people were at the final Dodgers game in Brooklyn's Ebbets Field, which resulted in a 2–0 win over the Pittsburgh Pirates on September 24, 1957. The Dodgers began play the next spring in Los Angeles, but Ebbets Field wasn't demolished until February 23, 1960. The Pirates were 9–1 winners over the Giants at the Polo Grounds on September 29, as 11,606 fans witnessed the team's last game before it moved to San Francisco. The Polo Grounds hosted the expansion New York Mets for two seasons, until wrecking crews went to work on April 10, 1964. The same wrecking ball, painted to look like a baseball, was used to destroy both ballparks. Coincidentally, apartment towers were built on the former sites of Ebbets Field and the Polo Grounds.

5.11　C. The Indians' 1948 AL pennant

The Cleveland Indians were tops in the AL in 1948, with a 97–58 record, and beat the Boston Braves in seven games to win the World Series. The Indians weren't, however, a threat to repeat. They started the 1949 season with a 12–17 record and eventually finished eight games back of the New York Yankees in third place. On September 23, the day after they were eliminated from post-season contention, owner Bill Veeck staged a funeral for the 1948 pennant. Veeck led the procession with a horse-drawn hearse in the pre-game ceremony. Manager Lou Boudreau and the rest of the coaching staff were pallbearers of the pine coffin. A cardboard tombstone read: 1948 Champs.

5.12 D. Tropicana Field, St. Petersburg

There were rink rats in St. Petersburg before there were bleacher bums. The National Hockey League's Tampa Bay Lightning opened its sophomore season at the Florida Suncoast Dome (a.k.a. the Thunderdome) after a year in the Florida State Fairgrounds' Expo Hall. An all-time NHL attendance record was set on April 23, 1996, when 28,183 saw game four of a playoff series against the Philadelphia Flyers. Hockey moved to the new Ice Palace in Tampa Bay the next season, and baseball didn't enter for good until March 31, 1998, when the Tampa Bay Devil Rays lost 11-6 to the Detroit Tigers at the renamed Tropicana Field. In 2000, it became the first major league ballpark to instal FieldTurf synthetic grass.

5.13 C. It landed in a swimming pool

Splish, splash! Mark Grace of the Chicago Cubs was the first player to hit a home run into the Sun Pool Party Pavilion's pool over the right center field wall at Phoenix's Bank One Ballpark. It's situated 415 feet from home plate. Grace's solo shot made a splash in the sixth inning against Diamondbacks pitcher Andy Benes. Devon White was the first Diamondback to make a splash on May 16, when he slapped a dinger into the pool in the first inning of a game against the Pittsburgh Pirates and pitcher Jason Schmidt.

5.14 D. Houston

The Astrodome did its job and kept the Astroturf dry on June 15, 1976. But a rainstorm that dropped ten inches on Houston streets kept the umpires and staff from getting to the stadium for a game between the Astros and the Pittsburgh Pirates. Both teams arrived, and so did 20 fans, who were treated to a free meal and rain checks to attend a future game. The "rain-in" was a first for a domed stadium and just the fourth time rain spoiled a game in the Astros' history: the first three came in the team's inaugural season, outdoors at Colt Stadium in 1962.

5.15 D. Seven games
The Minnesota Twins had "dome field" advantage during the 1987 World Series against the St. Louis Cardinals. The Twins won all four games in the first indoor fall classic at home in the Hubert H. Humphrey Metrodome, beginning with a 10–1 blowout in game one on October 17. They wrapped up the series in the same place on October 25 with a 4–2 score. Four years later, the Twins hosted the Braves in 1991's World Series, which also started and finished under the air-supported dome. Game seven was truly a classic, as the teams were tied with no score through nine innings. In the bottom of the tenth inning on October 27, pinch-hitter Gene Larkin hit a bases-loaded single into left field to bring Dan Gladden home for the Twins' second World Series championship.

5.16 A. None
Cy Young was shut out at home during the first World Series, at Huntington Avenue Baseball Grounds in Boston in 1903. The Boston Pilgrims defeated the Pittsburgh Pirates five games to three in the best-of-nine series, the first post-season face-off between the winners of the AL and the NL. Pittsburgh, the NL champion, challenged Boston to the championship. Young lost the opener to the Pirates' Deacon Phillippe 7–3 on October 1. But Young redeemed himself with wins in game five and seven. The Pilgrims clinched the title on October 13, 1903, with a 3–0 win. The ballpark had a capacity of 11,500 and was built on a former circus lot across the railway tracks from the Boston Braves' ballpark, South End Grounds. Huntington Avenue Baseball Grounds is now occupied by Northeastern University's indoor athletic facility. A statue of Young was unveiled in 1993 near the place where the pitching mound used to be.

5.17 D. The Astrodome
The Houston Astros lost their first and last meaningful games at the Astrodome, baseball's first domed ballpark. The Astros' regular

season debut there resulted in a 2–0 loss to the Philadelphia Phillies on April 12, 1965. The last major league game there was a 7–5 loss to the Atlanta Braves to end a NL divisional series on October 9, 1999. Original Astros owner Judge Roy Hofheinz dubbed the Astrodome "the eighth wonder of the world." Not only was it the first domed ballpark, it was also the first stadium with artificial turf. When outfielders complained they couldn't see the ball, the roof's 4,796 panes of glass were painted. But the grass below died. So the Monsanto company installed the first Astroturf artificial surface in 1966.

DID YOU KNOW?

New York Mets announcer Lindsey Nelson went where no man had gone before. At the Astrodome on April 28, 1965, Nelson watched a game between the Houston Astros and the Mets from a gondola suspended 208 feet above the infield. During the seventh and eighth innings, Nelson did play-by-play via walkie-talkie. The Astros beat the Mets 12–9.

5.18 A. Pete Rose

Some baseball purists were offended when the All-Star Game went indoors for the first time, on July 9, 1968, at the Astrodome in Houston. But there wasn't much offence to see when the NL blanked the AL 1–0 in the mid-summer classic. Thirty-seven-year-old Willie Mays started in place of the injured Pete Rose and scored the only run. Mays singled in the bottom of the first and advanced to second on Harmon Killebrew's fielding error. He got to third on Luis Tiant's wild pitch. His San Francisco Giants teammate Willie McCovey grounded into a double play, but that was all Mays needed to get home. The NL's six pitchers kept the AL to only three hits (all doubles) and walked none before a crowd of 48,321. Mays was the first person to win the All-Star MVP award twice. His first award came in 1963, in Cleveland.

5.19 B. 16.8

It took more than three years to build Seattle's Kingdome and only 16.8 seconds for it to implode. The concrete dome—baseball's second indoor ballpark, which opened in 1976—stood for almost 24 years, until 8:30 A.M. on March 26, 2000. Demolition experts used 4,461 pounds of explosives to collapse the 25,000-ton roof as the walls fell inward. Some say the Kingdome's demise began on July 19, 1994, when four acoustic tiles fell from the ceiling, forcing the postponement of an evening game. The same week, two Kingdome workers were killed when their crane broke. King County officials closed the Kingdome indefinitely for repairs, forcing the Mariners to spend the rest of the season on the road, until a players' strike stopped play. Fans and players were evacuated on May 2, 1996, when an earthquake hit during a game between the Mariners and Cleveland Indians. The Indians were leading 6–3 when the quake—which measured 4.8 on the Richter scale—struck at 9:04 P.M. The Indians were 6–4 winners when the game was completed the next day. The Mariners moved to their new home at Safeco Field on July 15, 1999.

Game Five

CRAZY QUOTES

So you think kids say the darnedest things? How about baseball people? Match the numbered quotes with the letters corresponding to the players, managers and owners who uttered these pearls of wisdom.

(*Answers are on page 120.*)

SPEAKER

A. Dan Quisenberry

B. Bob Uecker

C. Bo Belinsky

D. Jim Kern

E. Bill Veeck

F. George Brett

G. Ted Williams

H. George Steinbrenner

I. Joaquin Andujar

J. Dizzy Dean

K. Joe Adcock

L. Bob Aspromonte

M. Earl Weaver

N. Mel Ott

O. Rogers Hornsby

QUOTE

1. _____ "If a tie is like kissing your sister, losing is like kissing your grandmother with her teeth out."

2. _____ "If I'd known I was going to pitch a no-hitter today, I would have gotten a haircut."

3. _____ "I ain't what I used to be, but who the hell is?"

4. _____ "I've seen the future and it's much like the present, only longer."

72

5. _____ "Every time I sign a ball, and there have been thousands, I thank my good luck that I wasn't born Coveleski or Wambsgnass or Peckinpaugh."

6. _____ "I still think neckties are designed to get in your soup."

7. _____ "The way to catch a knuckleball is to wait until the ball stops rolling and then pick it up."

8. _____ "Bad baseball players make good managers."

9. _____ "You measure the value of a ballplayer by how many fannies he puts in the seats."

10. _____ "I have discovered, in 20 years of moving around a ballpark, that the knowledge of the game is usually in inverse proportion to the price of the seats."

11. _____ "Trying to sneak a pitch past Hank Aaron is like trying to sneak the sunrise past a rooster."

12. _____ "I'm working on a new pitch. It's called a strike."

13. _____ "I've heard of guys going 0-for-15, or 0-for-25, but I was 0-for-July."

14. _____ "There is one word in America that says it all, and that one word is 'You never know.'"

15. _____ "People ask me what I do in winter when there's no baseball. I'll tell you what I do: I stare out the window and wait for spring."

6

MAJOR MAYHEM

Most of the time, ballparks are places to go when you want to escape the daily grind. Sometimes, however, violence, greed, discrimination and generally naughty behavior can't be stopped at the turnstiles. Don't let the specter of mayhem bring you down in your quest for excellence.

(Answers are on page 78.)

6.1 What did Chicago Cubs center fielder Rick Monday stop on April 25, 1976?
A. The assault of an umpire
B. A streaker
C. The burning of the U.S. flag
D. A brawl

6.2 How much did a cup of beer cost at Cleveland's Municipal Stadium the night a riot caused an Indians' loss?
A. Five cents
B. Ten cents
C. 25 cents
D. One dollar

6.3 What substance on George Brett's bat caused a major controversy in a 1983 game at Yankee Stadium?
A. Petroleum jelly
B. Rosin
C. Pine tar
D. Adhesive tape

6.4 What kind of bird came crashing to its death on the field after it was hit by a Dave Winfield throw in Toronto?

A. A blue jay
B. An oriole
C. A seagull
D. A bald eagle

6.5 Which New York Yankee's tie-breaking home run won the 1976 American League championship and started a riot at Yankee Stadium?

A. Reggie Jackson
B. Thurman Munson
C. Chris Chambliss
D. Bucky Dent

6.6 What souvenir item given to fans at Dodger Stadium in 1995 led to a game's forfeit?

A. Beanie Babies
B. Beer mugs
C. Balls
D. Bats

6.7 What was found growing in the Anaheim Stadium outfield in the spring of 1976?

A. Marijuana plants
B. An orange tree
C. Poison ivy
D. Strawberries

6.8 How many fans were stung when a swarm of bees descended on Cincinnati's Riverfront Stadium on April 17, 1976?

A. One
B. Six
C. 12
D. 100

6.9 San Diego Padres owner Ray Kroc was criticized for doing what at the team's home opener in 1974?

A. Singing the national anthem
B. Managing the team
C. Speaking on the public address system
A. Throwing out the first pitch

6.10 What were two women doing that resulted in their ejection from a game at Dodger Stadium in 2000?

A. Swearing
B. Baring their breasts
C. Being drunk
D. Kissing

6.11 A fire in what part of Comiskey Park caused a delay in a 1974 Chicago White Sox game?

A. The home dugout
B. The visitor's clubhouse
C. The bullpens
D. The commissary popcorn machine

6.12 Fans who brought a certain item to Comiskey Park in a 1979 game were allowed to buy tickets for 98 cents. What was it?

A. A baseball glove
B. White socks
C. A disco record
D. A baseball cap

6.13 How much was Ty Cobb fined for attacking a heckler in New York on May 15, 1912?

A. $50
B. $100
C. $1,000
D. $10,000

6.14 How many Los Angeles Dodgers players were suspended in May 2000 because of a brawl at Wrigley Field?
A. Three
B. 12
C. 16
D. 19

6.15 What was the final play of the strike-shortened 1994 regular season?
A. A double play
B. A home run
C. A strikeout
D. A winning run walked home

6.16 What piece of equipment did San Francisco Giants pitcher Juan Marichal use to start a brawl in a 1965 game against the Los Angeles Dodgers?
A. A glove
B. A shoe
C. A bat
D. A hat

6.17 During a game in which city did Roberto Alomar spit in an umpire's face?
A. Toronto
B. Baltimore
C. Cleveland
D. San Diego

6.18 What was the jail sentence given a fan for jumping on Houston Astros right fielder Bill Spiers in 1999?
A. One day
B. One week
C. One month
D. 90 days

MAJOR MAYHEM
Answers

6.1 **C. The burning of the U.S. flag**

Americans were celebrating their country's bicentennial in 1976. They also celebrated Chicago Cub Rick Monday for his patriotism on Sunday, April 25, in Los Angeles. Monday saved the star-spangled banner from being torched right before their eyes in the outfield of Dodger Stadium. As Dodger Ted Sizemore was ready to bat in the bottom of the fourth inning, a man and a youth jumped onto the field in front of left fielder Jose Cardenal. One of them unfurled the U.S. flag, spread it out like a picnic blanket and began pouring a flammable substance on it. Monday ran to the scene and snatched the flag away. The crowd gave Monday a standing ovation and the stadium's message board read "Rick Monday, you made a great play." Monday was three-for-five with two runs and an RBI, but the Dodgers were 5–4 winners in ten innings. Back in Chicago, May 4 was declared Rick Monday day at Wrigley Field and Chicago mayor Richard Daley invited Monday to be grand marshal of the June 12 Flag Day parade. Monday finished the season in the Windy City before he was traded to Los Angeles, where he finished his career in 1984.

6.2 **B. Ten cents**

Never again will beer be sold for a dime a cup at a major league ballpark after what happened in Cleveland's Municipal Stadium on June 4, 1974. The promotion drew 25,134 people, who saw the Indians rally from a 5–3 deficit to tie the Texas Rangers with two men on base and two out in the top of the ninth. They also saw a woman try to kiss home plate umpire Larry McCoy and a naked man streak across the outfield, only to escape into the bleachers, where a police officer was waiting. Then they witnessed sheer chaos, after two youths jumped out of the right field stands and ran towards Texas right fielder Jeff Burroughs in an attempt to steal his cap. Players from both teams came to Burroughs's aid.

An estimated 5,000 fans spilled onto the field to join the melee. Umpiring crew chief Nestor Chylak suffered a cut on his right wrist and eventually ended the game because of the riot. He declared the Rangers 9–0 winners in the first major league forfeit since September 30, 1971. That's when the New York Yankees received a 9–0 win over the host Washington Senators, whose final home game was spoiled when fans took over the field. The Senators ended up in Arlington, Texas, the next season as the Rangers.

6.3   **C. Pine tar**

George Brett's home run at Yankee Stadium on July 24, 1983, was one of the most controversial in baseball history. The home run was fair, but home plate umpire Tom McClelland agreed with Yankees manager Billy Martin when he ruled that something on Brett's bat was foul. Pine tar, to be exact. The substance is used by players to improve their grip on the bat. With the Yankees ahead 4–3, Brett hit a two-run homer off reliever Goose Gossage in the ninth inning to give the Kansas City Royals a 5–4 advantage. Martin claimed Brett's bat was illegal because it contained pine tar on more than 18 inches of the bat from its base. McClelland called Brett out and reversed the score. Brett went berserk and had to be restrained as he bolted from the dugout in protest. AL president Lee MacPhail later overturned the call and let the home run stand because pine tar did not aid the distance of Brett's blast. But he ordered the game be resumed on August 18 with two out in the top of the ninth inning. Some 1,245 fans paid $2.50 to be at Yankee Stadium on what was a scheduled off-day. Martin wasn't finished: he protested Brett's home run by contending that Brett didn't touch all the bases. Umpire Dave Phillips came ready with a notarized letter to prove that Brett touched all bases. It took nine minutes and 41 seconds for the Royals to ratify their 5–4 result. Royals' batter Hal MacRae struck out to end the top of the ninth, while relief pitcher Dan Quisenberry retired the Yankees in order. Brett was notably absent from the make-up game.

6.4 C. A seagull

Dave Winfield hit 465 home runs in his 22-season career. He also killed one seagull. On August 4, 1983, the New York Yankees center fielder took to the field of Toronto's Exhibition Stadium for the bottom of the third inning. He played catch with left fielder Don Baylor until the Blue Jays were ready to bat. Finally, Winfield threw the ball to a ball boy but aimed it in front of a flying seagull, hoping to scare it. Instead, the ball struck the bird, which plummeted to the ground. The ball boy came to pick it up with a white towel. The crowd of 34,684 was shocked and booed Winfield throughout the rest of the game. The loudest boos came near the end, because Winfield had a homer and the game-winning RBI in the 3–1 New York victory. Winfield was arrested after the game and released on $500 bail. An August 12 court date was canceled, however, when prosecutor Norman Matusiak decided the death was accidental and dropped the animal cruelty charges. Toronto fans eventually forgave Winfield when his two-run, two-out double scored the winning run of the 1992 World Series for Toronto on October 24 against the Atlanta Braves.

6.5 C. Chris Chambliss

Chris Chambliss needed help from New York police to score the home run that sent the Yankees to the World Series for the first time in a dozen years on October 14, 1976. Chambliss led off the ninth inning by sending the first pitch offered by Kansas City Royals pitcher Mark Littell over the right-center field fence to break the 6–6 tie. The 56,821 fans at Yankee Stadium were ecstatic. Thousands of them poured onto the field to celebrate with Chambliss. He struggled through the masses around the bases and was nearly trampled. Finally, a police escort cleared the way for him to touch home plate and officially end the 7–6 game and the five-game series. The Yankees held a 6–3 lead in the eighth inning until George Brett tied the game on a three-run homer. The Yankees, however, were swept by the Cincinnati Reds in the World Series, which wrapped up a week later. Yankee

Stadium, which reopened on April 15, 1976, after two years and $45 million in renovations, underwent another $100,000 worth of repairs after the game.

DID YOU KNOW?

The SkyDome was topless on family day. And so were some women among the 30,139 fans on July 16, 2000, when the Toronto Blue Jays beat the New York Mets 7–3 at the ballpark with the retractable roof. Marty Cordova's first career grand slam for the Blue Jays was overshadowed by four women who showed up to promote a local adult bar. The quartet appeared in the window of a 348-room hotel inside the stadium wearing nothing but bikini shorts. They yelled and waved to grab the crowd's attention until hotel staff put an end to the display. Since the hotel opened in 1989, it has not been uncommon for hotel guests to purposely appear in various stages of undress in one of the 70 rooms with a view of the field.

6.6   C. Balls

It was ball day at Dodger Stadium on August 10, 1995, when many of the 53,361 fans tossed their free baseballs on the field to demonstrate their disgust at the umpires' calls. The St. Louis Cardinals led 2–1 in the bottom of the ninth when Dodgers leadoff batter Raul Mondesi struck out and was ejected for arguing with home plate umpire Jim Quick. Dodgers manager Tom Lasorda was also ejected. Fans threw so many baseballs at the field that the umpires ordered the Cardinals off the field and asked the grounds crew to clear the balls away. First-base umpire Bob Davidson eventually declared St. Louis the winner in the ninth inning under the forfeit rule. It wasn't the first "ball delay" of the game: there was also a six-minute interruption in the seventh inning. This was the first forfeited game since the infamous Disco Demolition Night cost the Chicago White Sox a win in 1979.

6.7 A. Marijuana plants
More than 400 baby marijuana plants were found growing wild in the Anaheim Stadium outfield. They likely were a legacy of a March 21, 1976, rock concert by The Who, which was attended by 55,000 fans, including 10,000 on the field. Stadium management ordered groundskeeper Joe Verdi to use herbicide on the plants and refuse any volunteers who wanted to help remove the "wacky tabacky." Repairs were completed just hours before the April 9 opening game, a 5–2 loss to the Oakland Athletics.

6.8 C. 12
A dozen fans were stung as a swarm of bees caused a 45-minute delay in Cincinnati during a nationally televised game between the San Francisco Giants and the Reds on April 17, 1976. The bees zeroed in on TV cameras near the Giants dugout. Members of the grounds crew sprayed the bees with water and fire extinguishers, but that did little to pacify the winged critters. Two fans, including an exterminator, located the queen bee and lured the swarm into a makeshift hive. The Reds eventually won the game 11–0 on the strength of home runs by Joe Morgan, George Foster and Ken Griffey Sr.

6.9 C. Speaking on the public address system
Chicago native Ray Kroc owned the McDonald's chain of fast food restaurants, known for the Big Mac hamburger. Kroc quickly became known for his big mouth on April 9, 1974. During the San Diego Padres' home opener at Jack Murphy Stadium, the team's new owner took the public address announcer's microphone. He made several impromptu and off-color comments to the 39,083 fans in the middle of the eighth inning. With the Houston Astros in command, Kroc apologized for the Padres' lacklustre play. "Ladies and gentlemen, I suffer with you," he said. But the fans were distracted by a male streaker, which Kroc responded to by yelling, "Get that streaker off the field, throw him in jail!" Kroc promised Padres fans that

better times were ahead. Ten years later, the Padres won their first NL championship. But Kroc wasn't around to see his team meet the eventual World Series champion Detroit Tigers: he died on January 14, 1984.

6.10   D. Kissing
Danielle Goldey and Meredith Kott were escorted out of Dodger Stadium on August 8, 2000, for kissing. They said they were at the game with a man and woman who also kissed, but the other couple was not ejected. Eight security guards escorted Goldey and Kott from the game after management responded to a fan's complaint. Dodgers team president Bob Graziano eventually apologized to the women, on August 23. The Dodgers pledged to donate 5,000 tickets to gay and lesbian organizations and to have employees undergo sensitivity training. Goldey and Kott were also invited to sit in box seats right behind home plate during a game.

6.11   D. The commissary popcorn machine
Where there was smoke on June 7, 1974, there was a fire. In a popcorn machine, to be precise. The "maize blaze" forced a 70-minute delay in the eighth inning of a game between the visiting Boston Red Sox and the host Chicago White Sox at Comiskey Park. The popcorn machine was in the stadium's commissary, in the right-field corner of the lower deck. About 3,000 fans escaped onto the field, and 11 people were injured by smoke inhalation. Seventy firemen arrived on the scene. The White Sox eventually won 8–6, before 15,173 fans.

6.12   C. A disco record
"Disco sucks" was a popular chant around Comiskey Park on July 12, 1979, when the first (and last) Disco Demolition Night happened. Fans who brought a disco record to the Chicago White Sox doubleheader against the Detroit Tigers were sold tickets for 98 cents each in a promotion sponsored by 98 WLUP,

a Chicago FM rock radio station. After the White Sox lost the first game 4–1, the records were gathered in a pile in center field and exploded with dynamite. More than 5,000 raucous fans flooded the field. When peace was restored, the grounds crew discovered that chunks of sod were missing and shards of vinyl records were bountiful. Umpire Dave Phillips postponed the game. AL president Lee MacPhail gave the Tigers a 9–0 forfeit victory the next day.

6.13 A. $50

Major league commissioner Ban Johnson fined Ty Cobb $50 after he served a ten-day suspension for jumping into the stands at New York's Hilltop Park and attacking fan Claude Lueker. Cobb claimed that Lueker, a press worker who was missing a hand, had called him a "half nigger" during the game. Cobb punched and kicked the man's body and head. Though Cobb wasn't known for his congeniality, his teammates did strike to protest the suspension. On May 18, the Detroit Tigers fielded a team of replacements and lost 24-2 to the Athletics in Philadelphia. Manager Hughie Jennings served as a pinch-hitter, while coach James "Deacon" McGuire went behind the plate and caught for Aloysius Travers. The 20-year-old's only appearance in the majors saw him give up 26 hits and strike out one batter. When Cobb finally returned May 26, he helped the Tigers beat the Chicago White Sox 6–2.

6.14 C. 16

Wrigley Field's nickname is the "Friendly Confines." But it wasn't a hospitable place for the visiting Los Angeles Dodgers on May 16, 2000. A fan hit Dodgers catcher Chad Kreuter in the head and absconded with his cap from the bullpen. Kreuter and at least six teammates jumped into the stands and fought with fans. The game was delayed nine minutes, and three fans were arrested and charged with disorderly conduct. Before the end of the month, major league baseball suspended and fined 16 players and three coaches from the Dodgers. However, a dozen of the suspensions were overturned on June 29, after the Major League Baseball Players' Association appealed. Kreuter's eight-game penalty was upheld.

6.15 C. A strikeout

When the Seattle Mariners game in Oakland against the Athletics ended around 1 A.M. on August 12, 1994, few people knew it would be the last game until the next April. The M's strikeout specialist, Randy Johnson, struck out A's pinch-hitter Ernie Young to end the 8–1 game. On September 14, major league baseball announced the World Series was canceled for the first time in history. At issue was the owners' desire to control skyrocketing player salaries. The strike lasted 234 days, until April 2, 1995, when owners agreed to the players' offer to return. A 144-game season got underway on April 25, when the Los Angeles Dodgers visited the Florida Marlins and won 8–7.

6.16 C. A bat

The rivalry between the Dodgers and Giants was no less intense on the West Coast than when both teams were in New York. In fact, things got downright ugly in San Francisco's Candlestick Park on August 22, 1965, as the teams engaged in a race for the NL pennant. The Giants beat the Los Angeles Dodgers 4–3 on the power of Willie Mays's three-run homer in the third inning. But the game was overshadowed by one of the ugliest incidents in baseball history. Giants pitcher Juan Marichal hit Dodgers' catcher Johnny Roseboro over the head three times with his bat. Marichal claimed Roseboro's toss to pitcher Sandy Koufax grazed his ear after an inside pitch by Koufax. The game was delayed 15 minutes as players brawled on the diamond. Marichal was suspended for eight games, fined $1,750 and prohibited from traveling with the team to play the Dodgers in early September. But the Dodgers had the last laugh when they won the pennant by two games and the World Series in seven games over the

Minnesota Twins. The incident was the only blemish on Marichal's 16-year major league career, which was celebrated in 1983 with induction into the Hall of Fame.

6.17   A. Toronto

Toronto's SkyDome was where Roberto Alomar experienced his best and worst moments in baseball. The member of the two-time World Series champion Blue Jays even lived in a hotel that overlooked the outfield. But it was at the SkyDome that Alomar's career was forever tainted, as a member of the Baltimore Orioles. Alomar spat in the face of umpire Jon Hirschbeck on September 27, 1996, after he was ejected for arguing a third strike in the first inning. The very next day, Alomar hit a tenth-inning home run to put the Orioles over the Blue Jays 3–2 and into the playoffs as the AL wildcard. When Alomar was finally suspended, it was for only five games, effective the start of the 1997 season. If Alomar wasn't the most-hated man in baseball for spitting at Hirschbeck, what he said later did the job. Alomar told reporters that the umpire suffered poor judgment because he was bitter over the death of his seven-year-old son from a rare disease called adrenoluekodystrophy.

6.18   D. 90 days

Houston Astros right-fielder Bill Spiers didn't know what hit him in Milwaukee's County Stadium on September 24, 1999. Spiers suffered a minor case of whiplash when a fan jumped out of the stands and onto his back. The fan, Berley W. Visgar, was sent to jail for 90 days and fined $1,000 on April 7, 2000, for jumping on Spiers. Visgar had been drinking beer and vodka. A witness testified that Visgar told fans around him that he would jump on a player's back or streak across the field if they would pay his fine.

Game Six

BUILD BILL VEECK'S BIO

Bill Veeck (1914–1986) changed the business of professional sports. The showman knew that he couldn't guarantee that the on-field product would always be exciting. But he knew how to build a show around it. Build your own mini-biography of the 1991 Hall of Famer. Arrange the major milestones of Veeck's life in order by matching the numbered statements with the letters corresponding to the correct year.

(*Answers are on page 121.*)

A. 1949   D. 1951   G. 1979   I. 1981
B. 1947   E. 1976   H. 1959   J. 1948
C. 1953   F. 1946

1. _____ Bill Veeck bought the Cleveland Indians at age 32.
2. _____ Signed the first black American Leaguer, Larry Doby.
3. _____ Signed Satchel Paige, the oldest rookie in the majors; drew a then-record 2.6 million fans. Indians won the World Series for the first time since 1920.
4. _____ Buried the 1948 AL pennant after the Indians were eliminated from playoff contention; sold the Indians.
5. _____ Bought the St. Louis Browns and sent three-foot-seven Eddie Gaedel to the plate as pinch-hitter.
6. _____ Sold the Browns, who moved to Baltimore and became the Orioles.
7. _____ Bought the Chicago White Sox.
8. _____ Reactivated Minnie Minoso, who became the first player to play in four decades.
9. _____ Staged Disco Demolition Night at Comiskey Park.
10. _____ Sold the Chicago White Sox.

7

MASCOTS AND MEMORIES

When you visit a ballpark, maybe you'll be lucky enough to catch a home run ball and have its hitter autograph the ball after the game. Or maybe you can leave just satisfied that you were able to root-root-root for the home team along with a cuddly mascot. No game is more fan friendly than baseball. You'll gain some fans if you can answer all these true or false questions correctly.

(Answers are on page 89.)

7.1 The Oakland Athletics' mascot is an acorn. **True or false?**

7.2 Snoopy was introduced as the Minnesota Twins' new mascot in 2000. **True or false?**

7.3 Cleveland Indians fans received a rabbit's foot before a 1951 game. **True or false?**

7.4 The Pittsburgh Pirates' parrot mascot was suspended for one game in 1987. **True or false?**

7.5 The Atlanta Braves hired a chimpanzee to sweep the bases in 1975. **True or false?**

7.6 Eddie Gaedel, the shortest major leaguer in history, walked in his only major league at-bat. **True or false?**

7.7 The Philadelphia Phillies' mascot, Phillie Phanatic, claims to be from the Galapagos Islands. **True or false?**

7.8 Schotzie, the Cincinnati Reds' mascot, was a poodle. **True or false?**

7.9 Max Patkin, the Clown Prince of Baseball, had a question mark instead of a number on his jersey. **True or false?**

7.10 The San Diego Chicken was originally sponsored by a radio station called KGB. **True or false?**

7.11 The Florida Marlins retired jersey number five before they had even played a game. **True or false?**

7.12 In August 1982, the Atlanta Braves went into a slump after removing mascot Chief Noc-A-Homa's teepee. **True or false?**

7.13 The owner of a Chicago tavern was not allowed to bring his billy goat into a World Series game at Wrigley Field in 1945. **True or false?**

7.14 Hockey legend Wayne Gretzky is a former owner of a Honus Wagner baseball card. **True or false?**

7.15 A comic book artist bought Mark McGwire's 70th home run ball of 1998. **True or false?**

MASCOTS AND MEMORIES
Answers

7.1 False
New York Giants manager John McGraw called the Philadelphia Athletics the "white elephants" of the American League. So Athletics manager Connie Mack cheekily adopted the elephant as the team's mascot, placing a likeness of the pachyderm on each player's sleeve. It proved lucky, because the team won the AL pennant in

1902. A blue elephant replaced the traditional A on the front of players' jerseys in 1920. When the team was sold to Charlie Finley and moved to Kansas City in the early 1960s, the elephant was out and a mule was in. The elephant returned for good in 1988. At opening night in 1997, the A's introduced Stomper the elephant mascot, who entertains fans at home games in Oakland's Network Associates Coliseum.

7.2   False
In 2000, cartoonist Charles Schulz and his "Peanuts" characters were saluted by the Baseball Hall of Fame in Cooperstown with a special exhibit, "You're in the Hall of Fame, Charlie Brown!" Schulz died on February 12, 2000, on the eve of the publication of his final "Peanuts" cartoon. Of the nearly 18,000 strips he produced, 10 per cent had a baseball theme. The Minnesota Twins opened their 40th season on April 3, 2000, at the Hubert H. Humphrey Metrodome by saluting the creations of Schulz, a Minneapolis native. Life-sized Charlie Brown threw out the ceremonial first pitch before a game against the Tampa Bay Devil Rays. On the same night, the Twins unveiled their new mascot, a bear named T.C.

7.3   True
The Cleveland Indians used a rabbit's foot to prevent New York Yankees pitcher Eddie Lopat from getting his 12th win in a row over the Indians on July 14, 1951. In fact, 40,000 rabbit's feet were given away to fans attending Municipal Stadium. One fan even gained access to the field and threw a black cat at Lopat. The hex worked and Lopat was an 8–2 loser, but he ended his career with 40 wins and 12 losses over the Indians.

7.4   True
The Pittsburgh Pirates Parrot was ejected from a game against the Los Angeles Dodgers in 1987. Umpire Fred Brocklander gave the parrot the heave-ho. The mascot, actually Tom Mosser, ques-

tioned Brocklander after a controversial fifth-inning call against the Pirates. Andy Van Slyke, the ump ruled, had trapped a line drive in a diving catch, even though the replays on the electronic scoreboard at Three Rivers Stadium supported Mosser. The Dodgers scored a three-run homer by Pedro Guerrero, which prompted Mosser to get on a three-wheeled motor scooter and throw a foam ball at the ump. Mosser flew with his motor scooter to an exit near the center field fence, but he didn't escape the long arm of the National League. He was suspended for one game.

7.5 True

Before the 1975 season, the Atlanta Braves hired a chimpanzee to sweep the bases at Atlanta–Fulton County Stadium after the fifth inning of each game. The Braves' front office received so many complaints from the public that the chimp was fired before it got a chance to do its job. The chimp was also supposed to clean up the shoes of the umpires and infielders.

7.6 True

On August 19, 1951, all three feet and seven inches of Eddie Gaedel came to the plate and walked to first base just once for the St. Louis Browns against the Detroit Tigers. Pitcher Bob Cain gave the 26-year-old Chicagoan four straight balls. Gaedel took advantage of his tiny strike zone. He didn't get beyond first, however. Pinch-hitter Jim Delsing replaced Gaedel in the first inning of the second half of a doubleheader. Browns owner Bill Veeck was responsible for Gaedel becoming the shortest player in major league history. Gaedel wore jersey number $1/8$ in the historic game.

7.7 True

The six-foot, 300-pound Phillie Phanatic, whose biography lists his birthplace as the Galapagos Islands, made his debut on April 25, 1978. The Phanatic has bright-green fur, white eyeballs with black pupils, purple eyelashes and blue eyebrows. His physical defects are listed as being overweight and having clumsy feet, an extra-long beak, a curled-up red tongue, a gawking neck and a slight case of body odor. The Phanatic has been to Japan and Australia as a goodwill ambassador for major league baseball.

7.8 False

Schotzie was the name of the Cincinnati Reds' mascot during the ownership tenure of Marge Schott. The St. Bernard dog was not popular with players, however; it often urinated or defecated on the field at Riverfront Stadium, where Schott insisted it be allowed during batting practice. Major league baseball eventually banned Schott's dog from the field. The original Schotzie died in 1991 and was replaced by Schotzie 02, whose other claim to fame was starring in the 1992 movie *Beethoven*.

7.9 True

Max Patkin died on October 30, 1999, at age 79, in Paoli, Pennsylvania. The Clown Prince of Baseball was known for his sideways baseball cap, vintage uniform and rubber face. He traveled the continent from the mid-1940s to the mid-1990s, appearing at ballparks big and small. He even played himself in the minor league blockbuster movie *Bull Durham*. Patkin was a right-handed pitcher who signed a professional contract with the Chicago White Sox in 1941. He compiled a 13–10 record in his first season with the Wisconsin Rapids, but eventually was assigned to a naval hospital in Hawaii during World War II. He kept playing baseball and one day pitched against Joe DiMaggio. Patkin struck out the Yankee Clipper the first time he came to bat. The next time, DiMaggio got his revenge with a home run blast. Patkin made light of the situation by mocking DiMaggio's trot around the bases. In 1946 Bill Veeck bought the Cleveland Indians and hired Patkin to coach first base and pitch during batting practice. Patkin's last game was in Reading, Pennsylvania, on August 19, 1995. His jersey, featuring "?" instead of a number, was given to the Hall of Fame.

7.10 True

Ted Giannoulas, a journalism student at San Diego State University, was hired by FM rock station KGB for $2 an hour to dress up in a chicken suit and give away chocolate Easter eggs at the San Diego Zoo in spring 1974. His next assignment as a promotional agent for KGB was to give Lynyrd Skynyrd and George Thorogood records to fans at San Diego Padres home games. When the booty ran out, the chicken didn't fly the coop. He stayed for the game, providing a welcome diversion from the Padres' dismal play. It wasn't until 1976 that he was allowed on field at Jack Murphy Stadium, where he performed routines between innings. His first involved picking a fight with an umpire. After being fired by KGB in 1979, Giannoulas won a lawsuit against the radio station and continued to work in a chicken suit at baseball games in the minors and majors around North America.

7.11 True

The Florida Marlins retired jersey number 5 before they played their first regular season game in history on April 5, 1993. The NL expansion team chose to honor late president and chief operating officer Carl Barger by retiring the number of his favorite baseball player, Joe DiMaggio. Barger died of a heart attack on December 9, 1992, at the Baseball Winter Meetings in Louisville, Kentucky. AL president Dr. Bobby Brown, a retired cardiac surgeon and former Yankee player, tried unsuccessfully to save Barger's life. The Marlins beat the Los Angeles Dodgers at Joe Robbie Stadium in Miami 6–3 before 42,334 fans. DiMaggio made the ceremonial first pitch.

7.12 True

The Atlanta Braves were in a pennant race and wanted to sell more tickets in Atlanta–Fulton County Stadium in August 1982. So they increased the seating capacity by 235 seats. By doing so, they sacrificed the teepee where mascot Chief Noc-A-Homa did a victory dance after home runs. The Braves lost 15 of 16 games, but the chief's tent was returned and the team recovered to win the pennant on the last day of the season.

7.13 True

Billy Goat Tavern owner Billy Sianis placed the famous "billy goat hex" on the Chicago Cubs when he was turned away from Wrigley Field with his pet billy goat during the 1945 World Series. Ushers cited the goat's odor. Sianis had already purchased tickets for himself and his goat, Murphy. After the Cubs lost to the Tigers, Sianis sent a telegram to owner Philip K. Wrigley: "Who stinks now." The year before he died in 1969, Sianis removed the hex. On July 4, 1973, Sianis's son, Sam, tried to bring his goat, Socrates, to Wrigley Field but was turned away by ushers. The younger Sianis reinstated the hex. Sianis and his goat were invited to remove the hex on opening day, when the Tribune Company bought the Cubs in 1982. The Cubs still haven't returned to the World Series, however.

7.14 True

A card featuring the great Pittsburgh Pirates shortstop Honus Wagner attracted a winning $1.1 million bid at an auction on July 15, 2000, on the eBay Internet auction Web site. Bidding had begun at $500,000 ten days earlier, and 13 bids were made. The buyer's identity was not disclosed. The card's previous owners included hockey legend Wayne Gretzky and a one-time owner of the Los Angeles Kings, Bruce McNall. Gretzky and McNall paid $461,000 for the card in 1991. The American Tobacco Company issued the card in 1909. The card was so rare because Wagner did not agree with his image being used to sell cigarettes.

7.15 True

The ball Mark McGwire hit for his record 70th home run of the 1998 season was purchased in a January 12, 1999, auction for $3.005 million, making it the most valuable baseball in history.

Phil Ozersky, a 26-year-old fan, caught the ball at Busch Stadium on September 27, 1998. Todd McFarlane, a Canadian comic book artist, film director and producer, bought the ball and made it the feature attraction of his touring McFarlane Collection. The exhibit included five other McGwire home run balls and two of Sammy Sosa's. McFarlane was born in Calgary, Alberta, in 1961 and wanted a career in the big leagues, but he broke his ankle sliding home in a game for Eastern Washington University. Instead, he settled for a bachelor's degree in fine arts and graphic design. The National Baseball Hall of Fame acquired the ball from McGwire's 62nd home run and the two bats he used to hammer the last 14 home runs of the historic season. Tim Forneris, a St. Louis Cardinals groundskeeper, retrieved the home run ball that put McGwire ahead of Roger Maris.

Game Seven

NICKNAMES SEARCH

Find the listed nicknames hidden in all directions in the following word search puzzle.

(Answers are on page 121.)

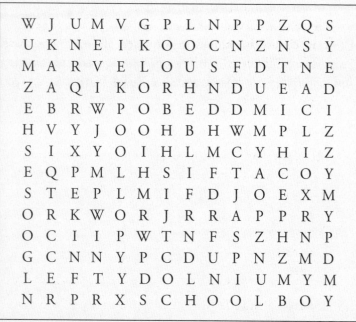

```
W  J  U  M  V  G  P  L  N  P  P  Z  Q  S
U  K  N  E  I  K  O  O  C  N  Z  N  S  Y
M  A  R  V  E  L  O  U  S  F  D  T  N  E
Z  A  Q  I  K  O  R  H  N  D  U  E  A  D
E  B  R  W  P  O  B  E  D  D  M  I  C  I
H  V  Y  J  O  O  H  B  H  W  M  P  L  Z
S  I  X  Y  O  I  H  L  M  C  Y  H  I  Z
E  Q  P  M  L  H  S  I  F  T  A  C  O  Y
S  T  E  P  L  M  I  F  D  J  O  E  X  M
O  R  K  W  O  R  J  R  R  A  P  P  R  Y
O  C  I  I  P  W  T  N  F  S  Z  H  N  P
G  C  N  N  Y  P  C  D  U  P  N  Z  M  D
L  E  F  T  Y  D  O  L  N  I  U  M  Y  M
N  R  P  R  X  S  C  H  O  O  L  B  O  Y
```

SEARCH WORDS

MARVELOUS Marv Throneberry
CATFISH Hunter
PIE Traynor
DAZZY Vance
DIZZY Dean
LEFTY Gomez
OILCAN Boyd
SCHOOLBOY Rowe

COOKIE Rojas
HIPPO Vaughn
BOOMER Wells
PUD Galvin
DUMMY Hoy
PREACHER Roe
GOOSE Gossage

8

FLICKS: BASEBALL ON SCREEN

Baseball is not only entertaining; it even has redeeming qualities. Case in point: in the 1989 contemporary classic baseball fantasy, *Field of Dreams*—the film adaptation of author W.P. Kinsella's novel *Shoeless Joe*—a second chance is granted to forgotten and disgraced baseball players (including "Shoeless" Joe Jackson) who mysteriously appear in a diamond carved from an Iowa farmer's cornfield. See if you can redeem yourself by answering the following questions correctly.

(Answers are on page 101.)

8.1 Which fielding position was not mentioned by the burlesque comedy duo Abbott and Costello in the classic "Who's On First?" routine?
   A. First base
   B. Shortstop
   C. Right field
   D. Pitcher

8.2 Joe DiMaggio and Marilyn Monroe were married for how many months when the blonde movie star filed for divorce?
   A. Six
   B. Nine
   C. Ten
   D. 12

8.3 Actor Tom Selleck and director Michael Moore are both known for wearing which team's baseball cap on the screen?

A. The New York Yankees

B. The Yomiuri Giants

C. The Montreal Expos

D. The Detroit Tigers

8.4 Scully is the last name of an *X-Files* character and a famous baseball play-by-play broadcaster. What is the first name of the broadcaster?

A. Vin

B. Red

C. Jerry

D. Joe

8.5 Who starred as Jackie Robinson in the movie *The Jackie Robinson Story*?

A. Louis Gossett Jr.

B. Jackie Robinson

C. Billy Wayne

D. Denzel Washington

8.6 What famous actor was found not guilty of a serious crime the same day the Seattle Mariners played their first playoff game?

A. Charlie Sheen

B. Gary Coleman

C. O.J. Simpson

D. Robert Downey Jr.

8.7 1060 West Addison Street was the address given by Elwood P. Blues in the movie *The Blues Brothers*. What big league ballpark is located at that address?

A. Comiskey Park

B. Yankee Stadium

C. Fenway Park

D. Wrigley Field

8.8 What sitcom star and future talk-show host ignited a nationwide controversy in the United States after her off-key version of "The Star-Spangled Banner" in July 1990?

A. Roseanne Barr

B. Carol Burnett

C. Joan Rivers

D. Rosie O'Donnell

8.9 How many Oscar nominations did the film *The Pride of the Yankees* receive?

A. One

B. Two

C. Three

D. Four

8.10 Disney remade *Angels in the Outfield* in 1994 with the Anaheim Angels. The original *Angels in the Outfield* featured which National League team?

A. The Los Angeles Dodgers

B. The New York Giants

C. The Pittsburgh Pirates

D. The Chicago Cubs

8.11 What was Ty Cobb's occupation in the 1916 movie *Somewhere in Georgia?*
A. A bank clerk
B. A janitor
C. An accountant
D. A lawyer

8.12 Which former U.S. president returned to the broadcast booth during the 1989 All-Star Game in Anaheim?
A. Richard Nixon
B. Gerald Ford
C. Ronald Reagan
D. Jimmy Carter

8.13 His performances in the films *It's a Wonderful Life* and *Mr. Smith Goes to Washington* captivated audiences. He did the same in *The Stratton Story,* a movie about a Chicago White Sox pitcher. Who is he?
A. Bob Hope
B. Bing Crosby
C. James Stewart
D. Jimmy Durante

8.14 The movie *Major League* is about the Cleveland Indians. Which American League stadium was the site for shooting?
A. Arlington Stadium
B. Cleveland Municipal Stadium
C. Milwaukee County Stadium
D. Anaheim Stadium

8.15 Who played Ty Cobb in a TV movie about Babe Ruth in 1991?
A. Kevin Costner
B. Pete Rose
C. Charlie Sheen
D. Tommy Lee Jones

8.16 Which Pittsburgh Pirate refused a chance to appear in the movie *The Odd Couple?*
A. Bill Mazeroski
B. Willie Stargell
C. Kent Tekulve
D. Roberto Clemente

8.17 The actor who portrayed which character on the sitcom *Cheers* tossed the first pitch at Fenway Park on the same day as the series' last show aired?
A. Cliff Clavin
B. Sam Malone
C. Dr. Frasier Crane
D. Woody the bartender

FLICKS: BASEBALL ON SCREEN
Answers

8.1 **C. Right field**
William "Bud" Abbott and Lou Costello had audiences rolling in the aisles with their famous "Who's On First?" routine when they teamed in 1936. The premise was simple: Abbott attempted to explain a baseball team's off-beat lineup to a perplexed Costello. But only eight of the nine positions are listed; right field was omitted. "Who's On First?" made its broadcast debut on the Kate Smith radio program on March 24, 1938, and aired on live TV for the first time on January 7, 1951, as part of NBC's *Colgate Comedy Hour*. It was such a hit that five years later, a gold record commemorating "Who's On First?" was put on display at the Baseball Hall of Fame in Cooperstown. For the record, the lineup goes like this: Who's on first, What's on second, I don't know is on third, and I don't give a darn is the shortstop. Why is the left fielder. Because is the center fielder. Today is catching, and Tomorrow is pitching.

8.2 B. Nine

The Yankee Clipper, Joe DiMaggio, had been retired for two full seasons but was still garnering headlines. DiMaggio married superstar Marilyn Monroe on January 14, 1954, in San Francisco. They had been married only 274 days before Monroe filed for divorce on October 5. DiMaggio's love for her continued until his death in 1999. Bouquets of red roses from DiMaggio regularly appeared at Monroe's crypt for decades after she died in 1962. DiMaggio had considered asking Monroe for a reconciliation, but she died of a drug overdose.

8.3 D. The Detroit Tigers

Michigan natives Michael Moore and Tom Selleck both wore Detroit Tigers caps as they rose to fame. Moore wore his throughout his critically acclaimed documentary *Roger and Me*. In the film, Moore pursued General Motors chairman Roger Smith after a GM plant was shut down in Moore's hometown of Flint. Selleck grew up in Detroit idolizing the Tigers. As Thomas Magnum in the TV series *Magnum P.I.*, a crime drama shot in Hawaii during the 1980s, Selleck wore a Tigers hat. In the 1992 movie *Mr. Baseball,* Selleck portrayed an ex–New York Yankee trying to reignite his career in Japan.

8.4 A. Vin

Vin Scully's voice has been synonymous with Dodgers games on radio since 1950, when the team was based in Brooklyn. Scully moved west to Los Angeles with the team in 1958 and was honored by the Baseball Hall of Fame in 1982 with the Ford C. Frick award, baseball's top award for broadcasters. *X-Files* creator (and Dodgers fan) Chris Carter named Dr. Dana Scully after Vin Scully because actress Gillian Anderson also has red hair. Vin Scully was a national TV star long before Anderson: he called major league games for CBS and NBC in the 1970s and 1980s. Carter took his admiration for Dodgers broadcasters one step further in 2000. He hired actor Robbie Patrick to portray FBI

Special Agent Ray Doggett. Jerry Doggett was Vin Scully's broadcast booth partner from 1977 to 1987.

DID YOU KNOW?

The first film of a baseball game was Thomas Edison's *The Ball Game* (1898). The one-reel, silent black-and-white film documented a match between amateur teams in New Jersey.

8.5   B. Jackie Robinson
Perhaps no one knew Jackie Robinson better than himself. So he starred as himself in the 1950 film *The Jackie Robinson Story.* His wife, Rachel, was played by Ruby Dee. Clyde Sukeforth, the Brooklyn Dodgers scout who discovered Robinson, was played by Billy Wayne, and the part of general manager Branch Rickey was played by Minor Watson.

8.6   C. O.J. Simpson
Dubbed "The Trial of the Century" by the media hordes, O.J. Simpson was acquitted of murdering his wife Nicole and her friend Ron Goldman in Los Angeles on October 3, 1995. The day before, the Seattle Mariners appeared in their first playoff game against the California Angels. Randy Johnson pitched a complete-game, three-hitter for the 9–1 Seattle win at the Kingdome. Johnson walked one and struck out a dozen against ex-M's ace Mark Langston in the one-game tie-breaker to decide the AL's wildcard. Simpson, a Pro Football Hall of Famer, appeared in the 1988 movie *Naked Gun: From the Files of Police Squad,* with slapstick master Leslie Nielsen. During a scene in which Simpson descends a grandstand aisle in a wheelchair, the Mariners are facing the Angels.

8.7   D. Wrigley Field
In *The Blues Brothers,* Elwood P. Blues (played by Dan Aykroyd) gives his home address as 1060 West Addison Street, Chicago.

That just so happens to be where Wrigley Field is located. Aykroyd co-starred with John Belushi (Joliet Jake Blues) in the spinoff from the popular *Saturday Night Live* TV comedy sketch.

8.8   A.   Roseanne Barr

Roseanne Barr "sang" "The Star-Spangled Banner" before a game between the Cincinnati Reds and San Diego Padres on July 25, 1990. Normally patriotic fans started booing the sitcom star as Barr screamed the anthem's words into the microphone. When she was finished, Barr grabbed her crotch and spat at the ground, like ballplayers have been known to do. The rendition ignited a national controversy. At the time, the Padres' chairman was Tom Werner, producer of Barr's TV series. Barr's co-star, John Goodman, portrayed Babe Ruth in a feature film biography, *The Babe,* in 1992.

8.9   B.   Two

The Pride of the Yankees (1942) was nominated for best picture at the Oscars; Teresa Wright was nominated for best actress. Lefty O'Doul tutored Gary Cooper, who played Lou Gehrig. Babe Herman, meanwhile, doubled for Cooper. The other, better-known Babe—Babe Ruth—played himself. Wrigley Field in Los Angeles was a site for shooting.

DID YOU KNOW?

Babe Ruth starred in two feature films: *Headin' Home* (1920) and *Babe Comes Home* (1927). Ruth made a cameo appearance in Harold Lloyd's 1928 comedy, *Speedy.*

8.10   C.   The Pittsburgh Pirates

The original *Angels in the Outfield,* released to theaters in 1951, was a fantasy that had angels looking over the Pittsburgh Pirates. Paul Douglas starred as Guffy McGovern, a manager of the sad-sack Pittsburgh Pirates who received some divine intervention. The film was shot at Forbes Field in Pittsburgh, with cameo appearances by Ty Cobb and Joe DiMaggio. Another cameo was by Bing Crosby, a part-owner of the Pirates at the time. The Pirates really did need angels to help their cause, but the movie didn't seem to help much. The Pirates were 57–96 in 1950 and improved to 64–90 the next season, but in 1952, a year after the film hit the theaters, the Pirates were a dismal 42–112 in regular-season play. The Angels had better luck. The year the remake was released, the team went 47–68; in 1995, the team went 78–67.

8.11 **A. A bank clerk**
Ty Cobb died a wealthy man in 1961 because of his post-baseball investments, not his brief acting career. In 1916 he starred in *Somewhere in Georgia* as a bank clerk who gets a lucky break and joins the Detroit Tigers.

8.12 **C. Ronald Reagan**
On July 11, 1989, former president Ronald Reagan joined NBC play-by-play announcer Vin Scully in the broadcast booth in the All-Star Game at Anaheim. Reagan did an inning of color commentary. He was enjoying his retirement from politics; his second term as president had ended earlier that year, when Vice-

---

DID YOU KNOW?

On October 1, 1951, the historic three-game NL playoff between the New York Giants and Brooklyn Dodgers began live on coast-to-coast TV. Ernie Harwell and Vin Scully on NBC joined Red Barber and Connie Desmond. The best-of-three ended with Giant Bobby Thomson's famous game (and series) winning "shot heard 'round the world" home run. Twenty years and 12 days later, the Baltimore Orioles and Pittsburgh Pirates met in the first prime-time World Series telecast, a 4–3 game four win by the Pirates before 61 million NBC viewers.

President George Bush succeeded him in the White House. Reagan had been a play-by-play broadcaster during the 1930s for radio station WHO in Des Moines, Iowa, before becoming a Hollywood actor. During his Hollywood career he portrayed Hall of Fame pitcher Grover Cleveland Alexander in the movie *The Winning Team*. Alexander, incidentally, had been named after an earlier U.S. president, Grover Cleveland.

8.13   C.   James Stewart

James Stewart starred as Chicago White Sox pitcher Monty Stratton, who lost a leg in a hunting accident in 1949's *The Stratton Story*. Stratton came back after the accident and was batting-practice pitcher for two years in Chicago before he attempted a comeback in 1946, in the Class C East Texas League. He was 36–23 in five seasons with Chicago. Stratton consulted with the cast and crew on set. Jimmy Dykes, Bill Dickey and Luke Appling are among the big leaguers who appeared in the movie, which won an Oscar for best screenplay.

8.14   C.   Milwaukee County Stadium

The Cleveland Indians' home park in the 1989 feature comedy *Major League* was actually County Stadium in Milwaukee. The film, starring Tom Berenger, Charlie Sheen and Corbin Bernsen, is about the Indians team that finally wins a pennant. Former major league catcher Bob Uecker, the Milwaukee Brewers' play-by-play broadcaster, appears as announcer Harry Doyle. Scenes

---

DID YOU KNOW?

The Seattle Mariners will always be number 1 in one category: the Internet. The Mariners were the first major league baseball team with a home page on the World Wide Web—www.mariners.org— and also the first to Webcast a game live, using streaming audio and video, in April 1997.

were also shot at Tucson's Hi Corbett Field, but only overhead shots of Cleveland's Municipal Stadium are used.

8.15 B. Pete Rose
Stephen Lang starred as Babe Ruth in the 1991 TV movie of the same name. The show was a composite of two biographies of Ruth. Pete Rose, who surpassed Ty Cobb in the all-time hit parade in 1985, had a cameo appearance as Cobb.

8.16 D. Roberto Clemente
The New York Mets led the Pittsburgh Pirates 1–0 in the top of the ninth, with none out and the bases loaded, when Bill Mazeroski hit into a triple play. The scene appeared in the movie *The Odd Couple,* but not on the official score sheet. It actually happened before a scheduled game in 1967. Sports writer Oscar Madison (Walter Matthau) missed the game-ending play from his perch in the Shea Stadium press box. Mazeroski hit into the triple play when Roberto Clemente turned down the chance for a taste of silver screen stardom. Clemente was to be paid only $100 and originally believed it was an educational film for children.

8.17 A. Cliff Clavin
John Ratzenberger (a.k.a. Cliff Clavin) tossed out the first pitch at a Red Sox–Blue Jays game at Fenway Park on May 19, 1993. Ratzenberger's character was the folksy, philosophical mailman with the thick New England accent who frequented the fictional Boston bar, Cheers. Ted Danson starred in the popular comedy about a neighborhood pub owned by an ex–Red Sox pitcher.

Game Eight

CROSSTOWN CROSSWORD

Crosstown World Series championships aren't common anymore. But when two teams from the same metropolitan area clash in the fall classic, it can simultaneously divide and unite a city. Here's your chance to unite the following clues with the correct answers.

(Solution on page 121.)

ACROSS

1. No intracity World Series was held in Boston, Los Angeles or _____ (12 letters).

4. In 1923, the Yankees beat the Giants 4–2, but lost 5–4 in the first World Series game at Yankee Stadium: "The House That _____ (4) Built."

7. The Dodgers beat the Yankees in the 1955 World Series—the last World Series win before moving to Los _____ (7).

8. In 1922, the Giants and the Yankees _____ (4) 3–3 in game two because of darkness. The Giants won the other four games to take the series.

9. The Cubs' famous infield combination: Tinker to Evers to _____ (6).

11. In 2000, the Yankees played the _____ (4) for the first time in a World Series.

12. The Oakland Athletics beat the San Francisco Giants in the _____ (3) Area series, which was interrupted by an earthquake.

DOWN

1. The Giants beat the Yankees in the first New York Subway Series in 1951. All games were played at the _____ (4) Grounds.

2. The 1941 Yankees meet and beat the Dodgers 4–1. The Dodgers were managed by Leo "The _____" (3) Durocher.

3. The St. _____ (5) Cardinals beat the St. Louis Browns in 1944 World Series at Sportsman's Park, where the Browns were the landlord.

5. The Polo Grounds and Yankee Stadium were separated by the _____ (6) River.

6. The White Sox beat the Cubs in the first _____ (9) World Series in Chicago in 1906.

10. The _____ (4) were favored in 1906 because they won a record 116 regular-season games.

9

POP HITS:
MUSIC IN BASEBALL

Baseball and music. It's a natural fit. Games begin with the national anthem, and in the middle of the seventh inning it's time to take a stretch and add your voice to the traditional singing of "Take Me Out to the Ball Game." It's like a hymn of thanks to the baseball gods, who have given such a great tradition for each generation to hand to the next. So keep singing the praises of baseball, long after you've correctly answered the last question of this chapter.

(Answers are on page 113.)

9.1 What former New York Yankee shortstop's voice can be heard on a hit song by Meat Loaf?
A. Tony Kubek
B. Bucky Dent
C. Leo Durocher
D. Phil Rizzuto

9.2 Detroit Tigers pitcher Bill Slayback collaborated with which famous play-by-play announcer on a song tribute to Hank Aaron?
A. Vin Scully
B. Red Barber
C. Ernie Harwell
D. Harry Caray

9.3 What jersey number did Garth Brooks wear during spring training with the New York Mets in 2000?
A. 33
B. 45
C. 38
D. 1

9.4 Harry Caray is best known as the Chicago Cubs' play-by-play man. Which major league team did he first call games for?
A. The St. Louis Cardinals
B. The Chicago White Sox
C. The Chicago Cubs
D. The Oakland Athletics

9.5 When did Congress make "The Star-Spangled Banner" the official national anthem of the United States?
A. 1918
B. 1931
C. 1945
D. 1976

9.6 A sign advertising a game by which team inspired a vaude-villian to write "Take Me Out to the Ball Game"?
A. The Brooklyn Dodgers
B. The New York Giants
C. The New York Mets
D. The New York Yankees

9.7 Which folksinger's rendition of "The Star-Spangled Banner" before game five of the 1968 World Series set off a nation-wide controversy?
A. Jose Feliciano
B. Bob Dylan
C. Pete Seeger
D. Arlo Guthrie

9.8 Which of the following is not a title of an album by
The Outfield?
A. *Play Deep*
B. *Diamond Days*
C. *Extra Innings*
D. *Wild Pitch*

9.9 Which famous record producer directed the orchestra that
played on "Say Hey (The Willie Mays Song)"?
A. Mutt Lange
B. Sir George Martin
C. David Foster
D. Quincy Jones

9.10 Actor Danny Kaye recorded a song about the Los Angeles
Dodgers in 1962. Which American League franchise did he
later co-own in the mid-1970s?
A. The Minnesota Twins
B. The Toronto Blue Jays
C. The Seattle Mariners
D. The California Angels

9.11 Indie rock group Yo La Tengo is based in which historic
baseball city?
A. Cooperstown, New York
B. Camden, New Jersey
C. Bronx, New York
D. Hoboken, New Jersey

9.12 Which late 1970s disco hit did the Pittsburgh Pirates adopt
as their theme song during the 1979 playoffs?
A. "We Are Family"
B. "Celebration"
C. "I Will Survive"
D. "Stayin' Alive"

9.13 What was the name of the 1960s band led by John Fogerty, whose baseball song "Centerfield" was a 1985 hit?

A. Canned Heat

B. Creedence Clearwater Revival

C. Country Joe and the Fish

D. Jefferson Airplane

9.14 What was the name of the Simon and Garfunkel song that referred to New York Yankees great Joe DiMaggio?

A. "Mrs. Robinson"

B. "Mr. Mantle"

C. "Mrs. Simon"

D. "Mrs. DiMaggio"

9.15 What instrument did Detroit Tigers pitcher Denny McLain play on two solo albums?

A. A guitar

B. Drums

C. The harmonica

D. An organ

9.16 At which stadium was Musical Depreciation Night held in 1951?

A. Yankee Stadium

B. Ebbets Field

C. Polo Grounds

D. Fenway Park

POP HITS: MUSIC IN BASEBALL
Answers

9.1   D. Phil Rizzuto

Meat Loaf's 1978 hit "Paradise by the Dashboard Light" includes 1994 Hall of Famer Phil Rizzuto in the background, doing play-by-play of the bottom of the ninth inning of a game. The song appeared on Meat Loaf's best-selling *Bat Out of Hell* album. Rizzuto spent his entire career with the Yankees, from 1941 to 1956. Nicknamed "The Scooter," Rizzuto was the AL's MVP in 1950, with a career-best .324 average. After his 1957 retirement, he became a full-time broadcaster and shared the microphone with veterans Mel Allen and Red Barber.

9.2 C. Ernie Harwell

Hank Aaron's pursuit of Babe Ruth's career home runs record inspired longtime Detroit Tigers' play-by-play man Ernie Harwell and right-handed pitcher Bill Slayback to collaborate on a tribute to the Atlanta Braves slugger. Harwell wrote the lyrics and Slayback penned the music and sang the ballad "Move Over, Babe (Here Comes Henry)." Slayback was 6–9 and appeared in 42 games for the Tigers during his three-season major league career from 1972 to 1974. Harwell began his major league play-by-play career covering the Brooklyn Dodgers in 1948. He called New York Giants and Baltimore Orioles games before moving to Detroit in 1960. Slayback isn't the only person to put a voice to Harwell's lyrics. Merilee Rush, Mitch Ryder and B.J. Thomas have also sung his songs.

DID YOU KNOW?

Babe Ruth was heralded as the greatest baseball player who ever lived. The Baltimore native was born on February 6, 1895, and died on August 16, 1948, in New York. Exactly 29 years later, on August 16, 1977, rock and roll legend Elvis Presley died in Memphis, Tennessee. Like Ruth, Presley is considered the greatest to practice his profession.

9.3 D. 1

Garth Brooks, outfielder, wore number 1 for the Mets—a number he's familiar with in the pop and country record charts. He spent spring training with the San Diego Padres in 1999 and hit

.045 in 15 Cactus League games. His only hit was at the expense of Mike Sirotka of the Chicago White Sox, on March 21, 1999. He made his debut a year earlier with the Padres as a pinch runner on March 15, 1998, against the Cubs, but didn't go anywhere because Greg Vaughn grounded into a double play. Only the Beatles have sold more albums than the switch-hitting Nashville resident—but none of the Fab Four played major league baseball.

9.4 **A. The St. Louis Cardinals**
Holy cow! Harry Caray spent 53 seasons in the broadcast booth, describing major league games for listeners and viewers of the St. Louis Cardinals, Oakland Athletics, Chicago White Sox and Chicago Cubs. Caray began his career in St. Louis, where he described Cards games for 25 years. He was known for his "It might be, it could be, it is a home run!" call and his catchphrase, "Holy cow!" Caray's son Skip and grandson Chip followed in his footsteps and also became baseball broadcasters. It wasn't until 1976 that Caray's tradition of singing "Take Me Out to the Ball Game" over the public address system began in Chicago, under White Sox owner Bill Veeck. His ten-year tenure with the White Sox ended in 1981, after Veeck sold the team to Jerry Reinsdorf and Eddie Einhorn. From then on, Caray became a fixture at Wrigley Field. After Caray's death in 1998, Cubs players wore a caricature of Caray on their right sleeve and the Cubs hosted a series of "guest conductors" to lead the Wrigley Field crowd in "Take Me Out to the Ball Game." Dutchie Caray, Caray's widow, was the first. Among those who followed were actor Bill Murray, basketball legend Michael Jordan, boxer George Foreman, Pearl Jam singer Eddie Vedder and Smashing Pumpkins singer Billy Corgan.

9.5 **B. 1931**
President Woodrow Wilson declared Francis Scott Key's 1814 composition "The Star-Spangled Banner" the U.S. national anthem in 1916. It took until March 3, 1931, for Congress to agree. The first documented case of the anthem's performance at

a major league game was game one of the 1918 World Series, on September 5, between the Chicago Cubs and Boston Red Sox at Wrigley Field in the seventh-inning stretch. The 19,274 fans were surprised to hear the anthem but quickly doffed their hats as the military band continued. The anthem was played at every game of the series and eventually became a tradition before the beginning of every major sporting event.

9.6   B. The New York Giants

Jack Norworth, a veteran vaudevillian, had never taken himself out to a ball game, but he wrote baseball's most-played and most-recorded song, "Take Me Out to the Ball Game," anyway. When Norworth wrote it in 1908, he had never seen a baseball game. He was inspired by a New York Giants subway billboard reading "Baseball Today—Polo Grounds." Albert von Tilzer put Norworth's lyrics to music, and the rest is history. Norworth didn't set foot in a ballpark until 1940, when he reportedly attended a Brooklyn Dodgers game at Ebbets Field

9.7   A. Jose Feliciano

Puerto Rico–born folksinger Jose Feliciano was enjoying the success of his lilting, Latin-flavored cover of the Doors' "Light My Fire" when Detroit Tigers play-by-play man Ernie Harwell invited him to sing the national anthem before a 1968 World Series game at Tiger Stadium. Feliciano was immensely honored to have the chance to sing "The Star-Spangled Banner" before Detroit met the St. Louis Cardinals on October 7 in game five. Feliciano, who had been in Las Vegas the previous night performing with Frank Sinatra at Caesar's Palace, walked onfield with his seeing-eye dog Trudy and sang a mellow, yet passionate, version of the national anthem. His dream soon turned into a nightmare: thousands of fans called the Tigers complaining that Feliciano had offended patriotic Americans by performing the anthem in a non-traditional style. The Tigers were 5-3 winners of the game and champions in seven, but some refused to forget about Feliciano. Times have changed. Nowadays, singers are encouraged to imprint their style on the national anthem—as long as they remember the words and don't sing out of tune.

9.8   D. *Wild Pitch*
Baseball, not cricket, was on the minds of a group of British musicians called the Baseball Boys, who began playing London nightclubs in the early 1980s. The rock band eventually changed its name to The Outfield and scored a number of hits on American rock radio beginning in 1985. The debut Outfield album, *Play Deep,* garnered heavy airplay on FM rock stations because of its hook-laden, melodic and highly produced sound. Later albums by the Outfield include *Diamond Days, Playing the Field, Big Innings* and *Extra Innings.*

9.9   D. Quincy Jones
The Treniers (featuring Willie Mays) recorded "Say Hey" in New York City on July 15, 1954. Mays put out another platter eight years later on the Duke label—a single of "My Sad Heart" and its flipside, "If You Love Me." Neither song was as successful as "Say Hey," partly because of Quincy Jones's work on the novelty single about the New York Giants outfielder. Jones started as a jazz trumpeter who played with jazzmen Ray Charles and Lionel Hampton. Eventually, he became a much sought-after producer and arranger for the likes of Frank Sinatra, Aretha Franklin and Michael Jackson.

9.10   C. The Seattle Mariners
Brooklyn native Danny Kaye (who was born David Daniel Korminski) recorded "D-O-D-G-E-R-S Song (Oh, Really? No, O'Malley)" in 1962 for Reprise records. Kaye eventually was a part of a six-man ownership group that founded the Seattle Mariners. The syndicate brought major league baseball back to the Pacific Northwest in 1977, after the 1969 expansion Seattle Pilots flew to Milwaukee and became the Brewers in 1970. Kaye's group held the team until 1981, when it was sold to George Argyros.

9.11 D. Hoboken, New Jersey

Yo la tengo is a Spanish phrase that, roughly translated, means "I've got it!" Venezuelan-born New York Mets shortstop Elio Chacon didn't speak any English when he came to the team and often collided in outfield with Richie Ashburn. So Ashburn was coached to say "Yo la tengo!" to signal Chacon to avoid trying to catch the ball. It didn't always work. Decades later, an indie rock band from the New York City suburb of Hoboken adopted the phrase as its name. Hoboken's Elysian Fields park was the scene of the first official "New York rules" baseball game, on June 19, 1846. The New York Knickerbockers lost 23–1 to the New York Base Ball Club in what may have been the first organized baseball match on record. Elysian Fields is now the site of a Heinz Foods factory. Hoboken was also the birthplace of actor/singer Frank Sinatra.

9.12 A. "We Are Family"

The 1979 Pittsburgh Pirates adopted Sister Sledge's disco hit "We Are Family" as their anthem during the World Series championship season. Willie "Pops" Stargell hit three home runs in the seven-game World Series triumph over the Baltimore Orioles. Sister Sledge reunited and performed the "The Star-Spangled Banner" at the Pirates' final game at Three Rivers Stadium, on October 1, 2000.

9.13 B. Creedence Clearwater Revival

John Fogerty's 1985 solo hit "Centerfield," which appears in the album of the same name, marked his return to prominence. He had led the 1960s "swamp rock" band Creedence Clearwater Revival but went solo in 1972. "Centerfield" paid tribute to Willie Mays, Ty Cobb and Joe DiMaggio, while celebrating baseball's rock and roll–like ability to keep one youthful.

9.14 A. "Mrs. Robinson"

Paul Simon, one half of the 1960s folk duo Simon and Garfunkel, performed a poignant solo version of "Mrs. Robinson" at

Yankee Stadium on April 25, 1999, in memory of Joe DiMaggio. The March 8 death of the "Yankee Clipper" was the reason for the memorial service before the Yankees' 4–3 win over the Toronto Blue Jays in 11 innings. The song alludes to DiMaggio's status as an American cultural icon. Artists as diverse as Frank Sinatra and the Lemonheads have covered "Mrs. Robinson." Simon's combination of baseball and song didn't end with that composition. Another Yankee great, Mickey Mantle, appeared in Simon's video for "Me and Julio Down by the Schoolyard." Simon and Garfunkel, originally known as Tom and Jerry, broke up in 1970. "Mrs. Robinson" was released in 1968 and appeared on the soundtrack of the movie *The Graduate,* starring Dustin Hoffman and Anne Bancroft.

9.15 D. An organ
Denny McLain is in the record books as the last pitcher to win 30 or more games. He did it in 1968, when he won 31 and lost six for the Detroit Tigers en route to the AL's MVP award and Cy Young Award. He also made two records playing an organ: *Denny McLain at the Organ* (1968) and *Denny McLain in Las Vegas* (1969). The albums earned McLain gigs in Las Vegas and on *The Ed Sullivan Show.* He even flew his own Cessna airplane, hence the moniker "Sky King." But a hedonistic off-season lifestyle eventually caught up with McLain. The Tigers' first $100,000 player was jailed and suspended in the 1970s and 1980s due to gun possession, cocaine smuggling, gambling and racketeering convictions.

9.16 B. Ebbets Field
The Brooklyn Dodgers had a light-hearted approach to music. In fact, they encouraged fans to make their own music, regardless of their skill level or what the music sounded like. On August 13, 1951, the Dodgers held Musical Depreciation Night, letting anyone with a musical instrument into Ebbets Field for free. Some 2,000 people took them up on the offer and stayed to watch the Dodgers beat the Boston Braves 7–6. One fan even brought a piano!

GAME ANSWERS

Game 1: Casey or Yogi?

1. A. Casey B. Yogi
2. A. Casey B. Yogi
3. A. Yogi B. Casey
4. A. Yogi B. Casey
5. A. Yogi B. Casey
6. A. Casey B. Yogi
7. A. Yogi B. Casey
8. A. Casey B. Yogi
9. A. Casey B. Yogi
10. A. Yogi B. Casey
11. A. Casey B. Yogi
12. A. Yogi B. Casey
13. A. Casey B. Yogi
14. A. Yogi B. Casey
    C. Casey D. Yogi

Game 2: Presidential Trivia

1. J
2. F
3. H
4. B
5. G
6. D
7. A
8. E
9. I
10. C

Game 3: Minor League Monikers

1. F
2. J
3. I
4. O
5. E
6. P
7. N
8. C
9. H
10. M
11. A
12. L
13. G
14. B
15. K
16. D

Game 4: Retired Jersey Numbers

Reggie JACKSON 44 (Yankees)
Ernie BANKS 14 (Cubs)
Roberto CLEMENTE 21 (Pirates)
Lou BROCK 20 (Cardinals)
Harold BAINES 3 (White Sox)
Willie STARGELL 8 (Pirates)
Hank AARON 44 (Braves)

Larry DOBY 14 (Indians)
Frank ROBINSON 20 (Orioles)
Tony OLIVA 6 (Twins)
Joe MORGAN 8 (Reds)
Willie MAYS 24 (Giants)
Don WILSON 40 (Astros)
Bob GIBSON 45 (Angels)

Arrange letters to spell: JACKIE ROBINSON
Sum of retired jersey numbers: 311
Subtract 269 for Robinson's jersey number: 42

Game 5: Crazy Quotes

1. F
2. C
3. J
4. A
5. N
6. G
7. B
8. M
9. H
10. E
11. K
12. D
13. L
14. I
15. O

Game 6: Build Bill Veeck's Bio

1. F   4. A   7. H   9. G
2. B   5. D   8. E   10. I
3. J   6. C

Game 7: Nicknames Search

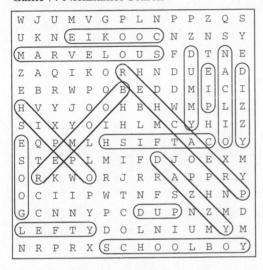

Game 8: Crosstown Crossword

ACKNOWLEDGEMENTS

The author gratefully acknowledges the help of publisher Rob Sanders, managing editor Terri Wershler, editor John Eerkes, designer Peter Cocking and the rest of the staff at Greystone Books; The National Baseball Hall of Fame Library; Peter Speck, Tim Renshaw, Michael Becker, Mick Maloney, Pat Karl, Lloyd Gell, Jeff Leyland, Joots Mistry, Ray Crosato, Brady Fotheringham, Christine Park, Robert Mackin Sr., Sherry Mackin, Jessica Mackin, Jonathan Mackin and you, the reader.

ABOUT THE AUTHOR

Bob Mackin is a sports writer and new media producer with additional expertise in coverage of business, politics and music—both popular and unpopular. The native of Vernon, British Columbia, has called Vancouver's North Shore home for much of his life. He was raised on Vancouver Canadians baseball. He eventually worked as press box assistant and substitute public address announcer. For four seasons he reported on C's games for the Canadian Press wire service. Bob's first book was *Record-Breaking Baseball Trivia,* published in 2000 by Greystone.